P9-BZS-267

African Fabrics

Ronke Luke-Boone

ncy 8690   746.096
                LUK

©2001 by Ronke Luke-Boone
All rights reserved.

No portion of this publication may be reproduced or transmitted in any form or by any means, elec-
tronic or mechanical, including photocopy, recording, or any information storage and retrieval sys-
tem, without permission in writing from the publisher, except by a reviewer who may quote brief
passages in a critical article or review to be printed in a magazine or newspaper, or electronically
transmitted on radio or television.

Published by

Krause Publications
700 East State Street
Iola, WI 54990-0001
Telephone (715) 445-2214
www.krause.com

Please call or write for our free catalog of publications. Our toll-free number to place an order or
obtain a free catalog is 800-258-0929 or please use our regular business telephone 715-445-2214
for editorial comment and further information.

Library of Congress Catalog Number 00-107842
ISBN 0-87341-914-6

Some products in this book are registered trademarks of their respective companies:
ABC Wax™
Armo®
ebay™
Folkwear®
Fray Chek™
Hibiscus™
Ivory®
Woolite®

Unless otherwise noted, all photographs by Ronke Luke-Boone.

Foreword

In our everyday world, fabric is often taken for granted because it's almost as prevalent as the air we breathe. It touches us constantly—protecting us, adorning us, and distinguishing us from one another. As a clothing maker and designer, however, my relationship with fabric is quite the opposite. In fact, I have an ongoing love affair with fabric. It's the essence of the garments I make and it supplies me with the inspiration for making them. I value fabric because of its exciting variations in color, texture, fiber, and design. And I marvel at its many forms, whether it's the product of nature or the laboratory. Fabric can be strong or delicate, utilitarian or luxurious.

In my explorations as a wearables artist and maker of pieced clothing, I use a variety of fabrics in my work, but I especially enjoy using ethnic fabrics from around the world because they bring a richness and individuality to every garment. These wonderful textiles offer more than just surface beauty with their extraordinary patterns and textures. They're filled with a sense of history and craftsmanship that reflects the pride and skill of their makers and has often been passed down through generations. Each ethnic fabric seems to have a story and an identifying feature that tells us where it came from. But because fabric is resilient and versatile, these textiles can live perfectly well outside of their own stories, making the transition from ancient cultures to contemporary lifestyles while still maintaining their integrity as they find their way into our modern garments, quilts, and decorations for the home.

The designs of Ronke Luke-Boone are a perfect example of the bridging of tradition and today. Her designs reflect her growing up in West Africa where she was surrounded by the textiles of her culture and where she came to cherish their history, appreciate the craftsmanship in their creation, and recognize the stories they represent. But her designs also reveal her love of contemporary fashion. From the very first time I saw them, I was struck by the fresh way in which she takes a fabric like mudcloth, for example, and uses it in fashionable little dresses, stylish jackets, and show-stopping coats. She is a woman after my own heart whose love affair with fabric and fashion has encouraged her to explore the possibilities that traditional ethnic fabrics provide.

Ronke has worked with all of these wonderful African fabrics and has learned to sew with them, discovering along the way that hand-loomed fabrics often have minds of their own. She has developed ways to tame their quirks with streamlined sewing methods that lead to successful results. And best of all, she shares what she has learned through the classes she teaches and now in this delightful book. Sewing is often a process of trial and error, and Ronke has done much of the testing for us. This book is a technical resource for anyone wanting to sew with authentic African textiles, but it's also a source for inspiration. It points us in new directions without letting go of the rich traditions.

Mary Ray
Associate Editor, *Threads Magazine*

Acknowledgments

"Enthusiasm begets enthusiasm"
Henry Wadsworth Longfellow, poet

This book is a dream come true. I have taught workshops on designing contemporary fashion with ethnic fabrics for several years. Many who have taken my class love African textiles but have no idea what to do with them. It has been rewarding to share ideas with them and see their creativity flourish; however, I can only reach a few people through my workshops. With this book, I hope I can share my knowledge with and inspire you.

Many people were critical in turning this dream into reality. First and foremost, I thank God; my courage to do much is anchored in my faith. I thank my parents, Elizabeth and Egerton, for inspiring me to sew as a child. Their decision to buy me endless yards of fabric to make party dresses, rather than buy them, was a stroke of genius. I also thank the men in my life—my husband, David, and my brothers, Olu, Kwame, and Emile—who form my fashion critique board and patiently listen to every "great new idea" I have. David, I also thank you for allowing me the space to explore my ideas. Olu, I thank you for sharpening my artistic eye and modeling. Kwame, you showed me that I can dare to dream big. Emile, I thank you for anchoring me in reality.

I shall remain forever indebted to my friends Karen Dove, Lisa Scott, Karina El-Halabi, Sharon Autrey, Chris Haggerty, Paula Cain, and Mohammed Bah for being so willing to help. Karen, Lisa, and Karina modeled, Sharon, Karina, and Chris illustrated my fashions, and Paula and Mohammed helped with sewing. Chris, thanks for your help with the cover design.

My gratitude goes to all who provided photographs: Doran H. Ross, Nestor Hernandez, Louise Meyer, Joan Baxter, John Nash, Wayne Kiltz, and Bosompin Kusi.

I thank Kim Johnson, Duane Pergerson, John Rusnak, Nestor Hernandez, and Ken Hong for photography. Thank you, Duane, for stepping in to model. Thanks to the guys at McLean Photo for your encouragement and great service.

I also thank Brenda Winstead, Dominik Cardella, and Lisa Shepard for loaning their designs. Thanks also to Trina Bowen and Toni Hurd for modeling.

My thanks to the following businesses for their assistance and encouragement: A. Brunnschweiler & Company (ABC Wax), G Street Fabrics, Miya Gallery, Quilts 'N Stuff, Curran Square Fabrics, West Africa Imports, Kente Cloth Festival, Inc., and www.african-crafts.com.

I thank my mother, Elizabeth, my brother, Emile, Laura Harris-Chwastyk, Moira Shaw, and Kwabena Smith for seeing me through difficult stretches. Thanks also to Louise Meyer, Madeline Shepperson, and Vernard Gray for all the wonderful discussions.

I thank my publisher, Krause, for believing in this project. I also thank Seiche Sanders and my editor Amy Tincher-Durik who were wonderful to work with.

The sleepless nights and hunger pangs were worthwhile to make this dream a reality, for now I

"Taste the joy that springs from labor"
Henry Wadsworth Longfellow, poet

Table of Contents

Introduction

I am fascinated by the textile and ornamental arts of "native peoples" around the world. The intricate details, the craftsmanship, the beauty of the work, and the stories the textiles and ornaments tell intrigue me. In many indigenous societies in Africa, Asia, and South America, the choice of colors and motifs in a textile are not always arbitrary or purely aesthetic; they may have meaning and tell stories of everyday life's struggles and joys.

For many years, I paid little attention to the work of textile artisans in my native Sierra Leone and other parts of Africa. They were simply things of everyday life that I used and took for granted. During my college years in Germany, I was drawn again to the textiles of Africa. With a new critical eye, I recognized the beauty of the work, appreciated the craftsmanship, and understood the cultural significance of the artifacts.

But I also love fashion. Clothes, accessories, and home décor are expressions of who we are. I challenged myself to use African textiles in modern fashions for my modern life. I'm on a wonderful fashion adventure. I consider my designs successful when I achieve perfect harmony between the textiles and design, each enhancing the beauty of the other, neither overpowering the other.

Using This Book

This book covers six of the most popular African fabrics available in North America and Europe: mudcloth, Kuba cloth, Kente cloth, Korhogo cloth, fancy prints, and wax prints. I share with you many of my design ideas featuring these fabrics. You'll see designs that are fashionable, functional, and fun! These are modern clothes, accessories, and home ideas that work for our modern Western lives. I hope you like what you see and are inspired.

If you've never worked with African fabrics, this book will give you tips, tricks, and techniques to help you get started. You will learn what to look for when you buy fabrics and how to sew and care for them. Take a second look at mudcloth, Kente cloth, and other popular African fabrics. If you can see these textiles simply as fabric and not "African fabrics," you will liberate yourself to use them in as wide a range of designs as possible. If you have experience with African fabrics, I hope that I enhance your knowledge and keep you excited. The designs I show here are but the tip of the iceberg—the design possibilities are endless. All you need to do is imagine!

I also hope that this book becomes a reference that you will use often. For each of the fabrics, I provide information about their cultural significance in relation to their African societies.

I believe that all of us in North America and Europe who love African fabrics form an important link to the African artisans who work very hard to make these fabrics but often have low standing in society. By supporting textile artisans, you play a critical role in strengthening the cultural heritage of their societies, in demonstrating that there is value (including monetary) in textile craft and expanding market opportunities for African textiles. The United States and Europe are huge growth markets for African textiles. While we respect the heritage of the fabrics, we should feel free to translate the cloth into designs that suit our Western lives. I hope this book is a glimpse into how our love for fashion continues to celebrate the work of many African textile artisans and may encourage them to keep faith with their textile traditions.

Enjoy!

Ronke

You Can Cut the Cloth!

Many who take my workshops say they can't bring themselves to cut up their African fabric. They are looking for designs that use the entire cloth; however, they admit that they find the African motif too strong to use the entire piece of fabric in one garment. It's a catch-22. You may be in this position, too. This reverence for the cloth is good, but it also limits your creative options.

African fabrics, no matter their close link to their respective cultures, are only fabrics. It is important for us to understand and respect the cultural heritage, but in order for the fabrics to live, we should interpret them into uses suitable for our modern lives. Showing modern uses for these old textiles plays an important role in showing the artisans that their craft has value and encouraging them to keep their traditions alive. (Note: I don't advise cutting museum-quality cloth. If you are not sure about your cloth's quality, get it appraised!)

1 Mudcloth

M udcloth was probably the most influential "ethnic" fabric of the 1990s—a pretty lofty thing to say about a fabric! But so far reaching has been this lowly cloth's influence, that today "chic" people (i.e. designers, public relations and marketing people) adorn everything from pillows and clothing to CD and book covers with motifs and colors of mudcloth to evoke an "ethnic" touch.

African Americans, black Europeans, and lifelong Africa-lovers immediately embraced mudcloth in the early 1990s when African traders started selling the cloth in the United States and Europe. For others, the rise of mudcloth coincided with lifestyle shifts in society when Europeans and Americans were embracing things natural, handmade, and ethnic. The Body Shop was in. Pesticides were bad. Organic food and biodegradable products were on the rise. Mudcloth—an old, traditional fabric handmade and hand-dyed using vegetable dyes which researchers date as far back as the twelfth century AD—echoed all of this influence. Unlike other African fabrics, the earth tones and geometric patterns of mudcloth were familiar and appealed to many uneasy or unfamiliar with things African. Chic people in Paris recognized mudcloth's aesthetic appeal, and designers quickly copied mudcloth's motifs and colors in collections with hip ethnic names. Today, textile manufacturers in Europe, North America, and Asia produce fabrics with mudcloth's familiar and appealing features.

AFRICA

Mudcloth comes from Mali, a landlocked country in West Africa, south of Algeria and partially in the Sahara. Its most famous city is Timbuktu, that once fabled place of far away.

Mali

Mudcloth in various colors and designs.

✗ Is There Really Mud in Mudcloth?

Yes, there really is mud in real mudcloth. The term mudcloth is the literal translation of *bogolanfini*, which is a cloth decorated by women in the Bamana-speaking region of Mali. In Bamanan language, *bogo* means "mud," and *lan* means "traces of." The most common bogolanfini cloth has white geometric designs against a black background. Bogolanfini is made through a long, complex process (which I shall only briefly describe).

✗ Making Mudcloth the Traditional Way

In traditional processes, women spin locally grown cotton into yarn. Men weave strips of plain white cloth using the hand-spun cotton on narrow band looms, and then they sew the narrow woven strips together to make larger pieces of plain cloth. Next, the cloth is washed to preshrink and dried in the sun. After the cloth is dry, women decorate it with dyes made from mud and leaves. Then, the cloth is soaked in a brown solution made from pounded leaves of the N'Galaman and N'Tjankara trees. The cloth turns bright yellow and is left in the sun to dry.

Once it is dry, the women can start the design process. The artisan decorates the cloth with geometric shapes that are often abstract renditions of everyday objects such as cowry shells. Using bamboo and other flat tools, an artisan outlines patterns she wishes to create and areas to be dyed with a fermented mud dye over the entire piece of cloth. Then she fills in patterns throughout the cloth. An interesting feature about bogolanfini is that it is the background, not the designs themselves, that is painted onto the cloth! The dyed cloth is then washed, leaving a black background, and designs, which stand out in yellow. The process of soaking the cloth in the leaf solution and applying the mud is slow and painstaking and may be repeated several times.

In the final stage, the artisan applies a solution containing caustic soda to the yellow areas of the cloth, turning them brown. The cloth is then left in the sun to bleach the brown areas white.

✗ Making Mudcloth the Contemporary Way

To keep up with the huge international demand for mudcloth, most of the cloth is made with simplified designs and modified dye techniques in a process that is much less complicated than that used in traditional production. First, farmers

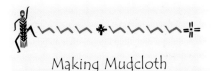

Making Mudcloth

* Women spin locally grown cotton into yarn.
* Men weave yarn into narrow cotton strips.
* Men stitch strips together into larger cloth.
* Women dye cloth with vegetable dyes.

A man weaving cloth on a modern loom.

Photo by Joan Baxter.

Fatoumata Coulibaly stirs mud dye while Fatoumata Ndiaye, secretary of the Widows Association, of Bamako, Mali, watches.

Photo by Joan Baxter.

Fatoumata Ndiaye stencils a design.

Photo by Joan Baxter.

Women painting designs on cloth.

Photo by Joan Baxter.

Completed mudcloth drying.

Photo by Joan Baxter.

grow the cotton. Next, men weave the narrow strips of plain white cloth on sophisticated looms and machine stitch the strips together to form larger pieces. Fishermen collect the river mud, and villagers provide the traditional leaves and bark used in the dye. Rather than leaving the *bogo* (mud dye) to ferment slowly, the women "quick" cook it in large pots. Using mud dye, women decorate the cloth with pre-cut stencils or by painting directly on the cloth. Cloth with multiple colors is allowed to dry after the application of each color.

Contemporary mudcloth is most commonly available in natural, black, brown, and mustard background colors, but I've also seen red, green, and purple mudcloth! These colors clearly indicate its influence and popularity in commercial markets. You can also find mudcloth decorated with scenes from village life, including farming, preparing meals, and celebrations instead of the usual geometric patterns.

Modern mudcloth in many designs and colors.

The Real McCoy

You can find factory-produced fabric called mudcloth with motifs inspired by the real thing, but don't be fooled: real mudcloth comes from Mali.

* There is nothing "even" or factory-looking about real mudcloth.
* It is hand woven and has an uneven weave. Its texture ranges from smooth to rugged, depending on the yarn.
* It consists of narrow strips sewn together.
* It is not sold by the yard off a bolt.
* It is a fairly stable cloth.
* Residual dyes will rub off before it is washed.

Manufactured mudcloth (top) and real mudcloth (bottom). Manufactured mudcloth is even-looking, while real mudcloth looks more hand-crafted.

Mudcloth's Resurgence

During Colonial rule, the French introduced their own ideas of style and relegated most local artifacts. After independence, mudcloth survived only in traditional circles in Mali; urban and educated people shunned it. In the late 1970s, urban attitudes toward mudcloth started to change, and leading artists began presenting mudcloth designs in their work. In 1979, a Malian designer working in Paris, Seydou Nourou Doumbia, included mudcloth fabrics in his winter collection, which was a runaway success. This was the turning point—a revival was underway. Literary societies emerged, new dyeing techniques were developed, and industrial production of the traditional cloth was launched. Within a decade, mudcloth had evolved from a shunned traditional artifact into a national symbol! What a truly remarkable transformation. Today, as a testament to its popularity, mudcloth is widely used for clothing and home furnishings in Mali and abroad and is copied worldwide in industrial textiles.

Popular mudcloth motifs and their meanings. 1. Mali 2. Mauritanian woman's cushion 3. Cowry shells 4. House of calabash flowers 5. Stream called the Wuowanyanko 6. Small drum 7. Samory's griot standing in the stream called the Wuowanyanko 8. Grasshopper neck 9. Tree leaves 10. Sickle 11. One twisted road

Source: Bokolanfini. Mud Cloth of the Bamana of Mali. Pascal James Imperato, Marli Shamir, African Arts, 1970

Where to Buy Mudcloth

- *Specialty (independent) fabric stores*
- *Bead stores*
- *Specialty galleries*
- *Museum shops*
- *Cultural festivals*
- *Mail-order sources*
- *Internet sites*

✗ Messages in the Cloth

The designs on mudcloth are not all random depictions; some are abstract and semi-abstract renditions of common objects. The artisan may cover the entire cloth with a single motif, or may create more complex designs with combinations of motifs. Some designs represent well-known historical events or pay homage to local heroes.

Here are some popular motifs (at left), and their meanings, used in mudcloth. Look for them the next time you buy cloth.

✗ Where to Buy Mudcloth

Mudcloth is readily available from specialty (independent) fabric stores, bead stores, specialty galleries, and stores that carry African and ethnic artifacts (i.e. museum shops) throughout the United States and Europe. Cultural festivals are also a good source for mudcloth. Mail-order sources for African fabrics may also carry mudcloth. On the Internet, do a keyword search for mudcloth to find vendors, or bid on auction sites like ebay. Buying mudcloth from mail-order or Internet sources has one drawback: the vendor selects cloth he or she thinks you would like! Because each cloth is unique, you may have preferred another piece, so make sure that you can return unwanted fabric.

Prices vary according to the size and quality. In the United States, expect to pay between $15 and $25 for small pieces (approximately 1 yard long) and upward from $45 for large pieces (1-1/2 to 2 yards long).

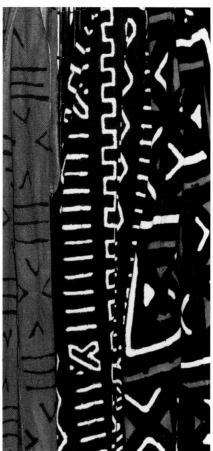

Mudcloth displayed at the Miya Gallery in Washington, D.C.

X Buying Mudcloth: What to Look for

When you buy mudcloth,
- Look for rippling and curving.
- Examine the color quality and overall aesthetics.
- Pay attention to the positions and repeats of the painted motifs.
- Buy enough cloth!

RIPPLING AND CURVING

Rippling occurs when the strips of mudcloth stretch, which typically happens when the basic white cloth is being made; however, stretching can occur at any stage in the production process, depending on how the cloth is handled. The fabric no longer lies flat and has a flutter or waves in it that can be subtle or very obvious. I often notice rippling at the outer edges of a piece, but I have also bought pieces with rippling within it.

Sometimes, the stretched strips not only ripple, but also curve. Curving can be so pronounced that the entire piece of cloth is distorted. You'll have difficulty laying a piece of curved mudcloth flat.

How do you spot rippling and curving? When it is very pronounced, it is easy to see. Lay the fabric flat on a large surface and closely examine it. Does it lie flat "naturally" throughout the surface? The fabric should form a rectangle, and you should not have to curve it to one side to get it to lie flat. Any curving indicates that the fabric is distorted. Think twice before buying it—you could be saving yourself a lot of frustration.

Stretched, curved cloth.

Excess fabric is pulled to make the cloth rectangular. Think twice before buying cloth like this.

Buying Mudcloth in Africa

If you are fortunate enough to go to Mali's capital, Bamako, you can find mudcloth everywhere tourists or visitors go. There are also major bogolan sellers in Bamako's main market. Outside of Bamako, travel to Segou, where there is a woman's cooperative that sells beautiful, good-quality mudcloth. You can also find it in Mopti and Djenne. The center of mudcloth production, however, is San, where women make the highest quality mudcloth. Keep in mind that you won't be alone when searching for mudcloth. Buyers from Japan, North America, and Europe buy and ship large quantities to satisfy market demand throughout the world.

COLOR QUALITY AND AESTHETICS

Aesthetics are personal; a cloth that appeals to you may not to someone else. However, some general issues to consider are: How well is the cloth dyed? Are the motifs crisp? Do the motifs please you? Look for evenly dyed cloth; sometimes the dye job is patchy. Look for color depth; select deep colors over "washed out" dye jobs. This is important because mudcloth fades with washing, and pale colors will fade quickly.

POSITIONS OF THE PAINTED MOTIFS

Motifs straddling the strips.

Sometimes motifs straddle two or more strips. These "straddling" motifs will be split if you separate the strips. Scrutinize the positions of the motifs. Will splitting the motifs detract from your design? Do important motifs straddle multiple strips? If you're unsure, you may want to buy extra fabric.

REPEATS IN THE MUDCLOTH

Because mudcloth is handmade, the artisan's discretion comes into play. While this gives the fabric its charm, it can also be a source of frustration when cutting and matching seams. The artisan may not position the motifs in a constant repeat, or there may not be a repeat at all. When you buy mudcloth, you need to study it closely and account for the presence or absence of a repeat in the motif. When in doubt, buy extra fabric for matching motifs.

BUYING ENOUGH CLOTH

Mudcloth is sold in pieces, not by the yard. Pieces typically come in two sizes: the smaller pieces are about 1 yard long, while the larger pieces are 1-1/2 to 2 yards long, but there is nothing hard and fast about these lengths. The width of each piece depends on the width of the strips (which typically range between 3-1/2" and 4-1/2") and the number of strips stitched together to make up the cloth (usually between five and seven for smaller pieces, ten for larger pieces). Much depends on what the artisan was thinking at the time he created the cloth. Each piece is unique, so you may not be able to get more later if you need to match dye quality or motifs or account for repeats, so make sure you buy enough cloth.

Buy Mudcloth That

* Lies flat on a work surface, forms a rectangle, and does not curve.
* Has even color quality.
* Has distinct motifs with clear lines.
* Is made of strips of similar quality.
* Has motifs that combine well with other fabrics you're using, if applicable (see page 20).

Remember: Mudcloth is sold in pieces not by the yard, so buy enough!

SHOULD YOU PREWASH?

Prewashing will take care of preshrinking. To preshrink, wash or dry clean mudcloth before you sew to reduce shrinkage and remove excess dye and grit accumulated during production and shipping. (See page 18 for guidance on washing and dry cleaning.)

DO YOU HAVE ENOUGH CLOTH?

This is an obvious question that has more relevance than with factory-made fabrics. With factory-made fabric, you can probably buy more from your source provided it's not sold out, but because mudcloth comes in one-of-a-kind pieces, stock at local stores may not be large, so you may be out of luck if you run out. Therefore, lay out all of your pattern pieces before you cut your mudcloth.

SECURING THE STRIPS

Mudcloth's narrow strips are either whip or machine stitched (straight and zigzag) together. If your pattern pieces cover multiple strips, secure them together before you cut. Here are several methods for securing strips:

• Fuse interfacing to the back of the entire piece of mudcloth (note how interfacing affects the fabric's hand). Armo weft works well.
• Fuse interfacing only along the joins of the strips.
• Whip or machine stitch over the existing stitches.
• Stitch the pieces together with a narrow seam on the wrong side, or use decorative stitches instead of regular machine stitching.
• Serge the strips together.

Before You Cut

Now you're ready to think about cutting. Here are some things to consider:
* *Should you prewash?*
* *Do you have enough cloth?*
* *Are the strips secure?*
* *How will you lay out the pattern?*
* *Are there rippled, stretched, or distorted areas?*
* *Are you happy with the motif positions?*

Lay Out All of the Pattern Pieces Before You Cut

I learned this lesson the hard way. I found this great piece of unusual mudcloth and decided a shift dress would be perfect. Blinded by enthusiasm, I laid out the dress front pattern and cut. I realized after I cut the front that I didn't have enough to cut out the back!

Strips secured with decorative stitching.

Interfacing is fused to the mudcloth before cutting the pattern piece.

Here are some things to consider when laying out your pattern:
- Avoid ripped, curved, distorted areas. The fabric in these areas has stretched and will show in your garment.
- Move the pattern pieces until you are happy with motif positions.
- Cut on a single layer when cutting large patterns or when matching motifs.

✗ Sewing Mudcloth Without a Walking Foot

Mudcloth may stretch as you sew. The degree of stretching varies with each piece of fabric. Use a walking foot or dual (differential) feed mechanism on your machine if you have one; it controls the slipping and stretching and you don't have to go through the process outlined below. Don't worry if you don't have a walking foot or a dual feed mechanism; the techniques described below assume you are working with a regular presser foot.

✗ Sewing Mudcloth to Other Fabrics

It's easy to prevent stretching and slipping when you sew mudcloth to other fabrics such as linen or cotton. Simply put the mudcloth on the bottom, in contact with the machine's feed dogs. This is important: the non-mudcloth fabric (i.e. cotton or linen) should face you. You should have no more stretching when you stitch.

✗ Sewing Two Layers of Mudcloth

Here are some simple solutions to prevent stretching if you don't have a walking foot.

Strips of Armo weft interfacing are fused to the mudcloth's

• **The fusible interfacing method.** Fuse narrow strips of lightweight interfacing (i.e. Armo weft) along the mudcloth's seamline. Stitch using an even speed. The interfacing stabilizes the seamline. With sew-in interfacing, follow the guidelines for seam binding on the next page.

• **Seam binding, stay tape, or tear-away stabilizer method.** First, mark the stitching line on one of the two mudcloth pieces to be sewn together. Second, center the seam binding (or stay tape or tear-away stabilizer) over the seamline you've marked. The piece with the seam binding should face you and the plain mudcloth is against the feed teeth. The seam binding, not mudcloth, is in contact with your machine's presser foot as you sew. You should have no stretching. Remove tear-away stabilizer once pieces are sewn together.

Seam binding on mudcloth.

SEWING NOTIONS AND OTHER THINGS

Here are some useful notions and other considerations for sewing mudcloth.
- Needle. Universal 70/10, 80/12, 90/14, or 100/16, depending on the fabric's thickness.
- Thread. Cotton-covered polyester for medium-weight fabrics, polyester for heavy-weight fabrics.
- Interfacing. Sew-in or fusible interfacing suitable for medium-weight and heavy fabrics.
- Seam Finishing. Use a zigzag stitch or serging.

The top edge is finished with serging and the right edge is finished with a zigzag stitch.

Mudcloth with different interfacings: craft interfacing (top), Armo weft (bottom right), and shirt shaper interfacing (bottom left).

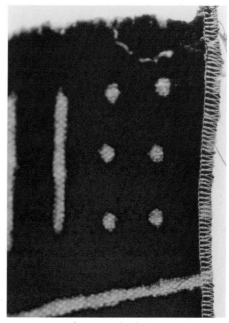

Front view of a serged edge.

X Caring for Mudcloth

Mudcloth is made from natural materials using traditional techniques and require extra care. The International Fabricare Institute suggests dry cleaning as the safest care method, but I've read other expert advice that recommends to hand wash it in mild detergent and warm water and not to dry clean or machine wash. I have washed and dry cleaned mudcloth and have been satisfied with the results of both methods. I suggest testing a swatch before proceeding with either method. Also, as stated on page 15, prewash mudcloth before sewing and wash it before storing.

To machine wash mudcloth, put it in a lingerie bag, set the machine on a gentle cycle, and use cold water and a gentle laundry soap (i.e. Ivory).

Mudcloth fades over time with washing and dry cleaning, so you may notice slight or marked fading after the first washing or dry cleaning, depending on the dye quality. Plan for this fading in your design.

Lay mudcloth flat or hang to dry. Over time, washing leaves mudcloth with a soft feel that I find delightful to the touch. You can press it once it's dry.

PRESSING

Mudcloth presses very nicely! Press as you sew. Lots of steam helps you shape and mold the fabric, but dry irons can also be used. Seams can be pressed open; however, expect some bulk because mudcloth is a heavy fabric.

STORING MUDCLOTH

There are no special considerations for storing mudcloth; simply fold it up and store it with your fabric stash. I advise washing or cleaning your fabric before storing to remove dirt and excess dye.

Mudcloth Can Be

* Hand washed
* Machine washed
* Dry cleaned

Expect fading and some shrinking with all methods.

X Design Ideas

Now we're at the fun part. Mudcloth is inexpensive and readily available, so you may find yourself working with it often. People exercise great freedom with mudcloth, using it in everything from hats, bags, dresses, and skirts, to coats, vests, pillows, place settings, and other craft items. Just be creative!

SELECTING PATTERNS

Because of its weight, mudcloth is suitable for structured and softly structured clothing, including skirts, coats, jackets, and vests. Select patterns without bulk. Avoid or alter patterns to remove darts. If you can't avoid darts, slash stitched darts and press them open. Replace facings with seam bindings or cut facings out of matching, lighter weight fabrics.

You can design fashions with a little or a lot of mudcloth. Think of using mudcloth in areas such as pockets, collars, and decorative bands.

For information about creating and altering patterns see How to Make Sewing Patterns, *by Donald H. McCunn, Design Enterprises of San Francisco, 1996.*

WHICH COMES FIRST: BUYING FABRIC OR SELECTING A PATTERN?

The chicken and egg problem. I have no hard and fast rule for this. For some, it is easier to buy the fabric first and then select a pattern, but for others, the reverse works better. The bottom line? Do whatever works for you!

LINING

Mudcloth softens over time; however, depending on the cotton quality, the cloth can feel rough against the skin. Consider lining your garments with rayon, cotton, corduroy, or synthetic linings. For example, I have lined vests with cotton, coats with corduroy, and dresses with rayon and acetate. The choice of lining depends on the garment and personal preference.

COMBINING MUDCLOTH MOTIFS

If you combine several pieces of mudcloth with different motifs in one garment, here are two things to consider. First, are the motifs complementary? You may find too many strong, random motifs in one garment jarring. Second, do the motifs repeat? How will the repeat affect your final design?

Mudcloth pockets on a linen jacket (Butterick 4642).

Model: Lisa Scott.
Photo by Kim Johnson.

This jacket features mudcloth detail its on collar, buttons, and pockets.

Photo by Kim Johnson.

COMBINING MUDCLOTH WITH OTHER FABRICS

Mudcloth has weight and combines well with other fabrics with visible texture and weight, such as Korhogo cloth, linen, hemp, and wool crepe. I have also combined mudcloth with chiffon to create pretty dresses. I'll admit that it does take a certain amount of creative thinking to visualize mudcloth and chiffon, but believe me, it can be done (see page 24 for examples).

COMBINING MUDCLOTH WITH KORHOGO CLOTH

The basic cottons used to make Korhogo cloth and mudcloth are produced by similar methods, so you can combine the fabrics in one project. I have seen this done in clothing and home furnishings such as wall hangings. Consider these two things if you combine the two. First, are the motifs complementary? Second, is the visual result pleasing? (Taking color, texture, and motifs into consideration.)

COLLARS, CUFFS, AND POCKETS

You can design fashions with a little or a lot of mudcloth. If you have a little, try using mudcloth as an accent in such areas as collars, cuffs, and pockets. This is a great, "safe" way to incorporate mudcloth into your wardrobe.

VESTS, COATS, AND CASUAL WEAR

Mudcloth makes great vests for the whole family, and you won't need much cloth for an entire garment. For spectacular vests, use unusual mudcloth with smaller motifs. You can use a pretty contrasting cotton, linen, or hemp to make a reversible vest. For reversible winter vests, consider using fleece, flannel, or corduroy for the lining. Think of other features such as a drawstring or elastic at the waistline, and play with fancy button and zipper closures. (See page 117 for instructions on how to make a mudcloth vest.)

Mudcloth is heavy enough to be used in coats—make a statement with these graphic fabrics. Remember the tips about complementary motifs and repeats when combining several pieces of mudcloth into a garment (see page 19). Corduroy and flannel make good coat linings.

Design by Ronke Luke-Boone. Model: Lisa Scott. Photo by John Rusnak.

Courtesy Lisa Shepard. Model: Karen Dove. Photos by Kim Johnson.

The dramatic Nomad Coat (Hibiscus Pattern 1003) combines two mudcloth motifs, raw silk, and corduroy.

Back view of the mudcloth swing coat.

Mudcloth swing coat trimmed with faux sheared beaver and faux leather.

Design by Ronke Luke-Boone. Models: Karen Dove, Karina El-Halabi, and Lisa Scott. Photo by Kim Johnson.

City Vest (Hibiscus Pattern 1002) is a great vest for year 'round fashion when made of mudcloth: wear it over a T-shirt or tank top in summer and a sweater in winter.

Model: Olu Luke.

Mudcloth works well with linen to make a tasteful man's vest.

Illustration by Sharon Autrey.

Mudcloth makes fashionable sportswear for men.

Illustration by Sharon Autrey.

Design by Ronke Luke-Boone. Models: Lisa Scott, Karina El-Halabi, and Karen Dove. Photo by Kim Johnson.

The Weekend Shift (Hibiscus Pattern 1001) made of mudcloth, linen, and raw silk (left), mudcloth and wool crepe (center), and Korhogo cloth and linen (right).

Design by Ronke Luke-Boone. Model: Lisa Scott. Photo by John Rusnak.

The Weekend Shift (Hibiscus Pattern 1001) made out of mudcloth and wool crepe.

DRESSES AND SUITS

Mudcloth can also be used in attractive dresses and smart suits. The Weekend Shift (Hibiscus Pattern 1001) is a striking, yet simple, dress. In creating this design, I was inspired by the loose-fitting caftan style in Africa, modern art, and the famous Mondrian dress! The color block works well with the linear silhouette. (A color block is a design concept in which a garment section, like a dress or jacket front, is divided into segments or blocks, which are in turn cut out of contrasting colors.) Although I used mudcloth sparingly, the effect is quite spectacular, resulting in a very contemporary dress.

Design Insight

◈ *Mudcloth works very well for color blocking. Select strips that offer great design effects.*

◈ *Less is more. Using mudcloth sparingly achieves a stunning effect.*

◈ *Wool crepe, linen, and raw silk balance well with mudcloth, because of their weight and texture.*

The Weekend Shift shown at left is made out of mudcloth and wool crepe. The mudcloth contrasts with the red fabric and balances with the black.

The Sleek Sheath (Hibiscus Pattern 1000; below left) is another striking, yet simple, dress. In this design, I took advantage of mudcloth's bold, graphic motifs. When laid against the solid background, the mudcloth motifs stand out and turn a simple sheath dress into a stunning number. Shown here in linen, this dress can be made out of wool crepe, raw silk, or hemp.

Here's another adorable dress (below right). Mudcloth and wool crepe are alternated in the bodice for a striking effect.

Design by Ronke Luke-Boone. Model: Lisa Scott. Photo by John Rusnak.

The Sleek Sheath made out of linen and mudcloth.

Model: Lisa Scott. Photo by John Rusnak.

Mudcloth and wool crepe look modern in this interpretation of Vogue 1587.

In this sweet summer two-piece (shown at right), mudcloth and linen are alternated. Wooden buttons and fringe at the hem are additional ethnic touches.

Design by Ronke Luke-Boone. Model: Karina El-Halabi. Photo by Kim Johnson.

Mudcloth and linen summer two-piece.

This Summer Sassy Number (at left) shows that mudcloth can go high fashion! In this sexy mudcloth and linen dress, geometry is fun. I used two pieces of mudcloth, one with squares, the other with Xs. I off-set the squares and Xs against curving, sweeping seamlines that draw your eye through the body from top to bottom. A tassel above the side slit adds provocative detail.

Design by Ronke Luke-Boone. Model: Lisa Scott. Photo by John Rusnak.

The Summer Sassy Number shows mudcloth and linen in a high-fashion style.

Design Insight

- "Ethnic" doesn't exclude high fashion—be dramatic.
- Combine mudcloth motifs skillfully by insight and understanding color and pattern design.
- Incorporate seamlines into design detail.

American interest in mudcloth is encouraging Malian artists to create more colors including red, green, and violet. In this adorable outfit that evokes the style of West African dress, Brenda Winstead, a Washington, D.C.-based designer, worked with a Malian artisan to produce this fresh, upbeat powder blue cloth.

Design by Brenda Winstead. Model: Karen Dove. Photo by Kim Johnson.

Colored mudcloth in a modern interpretation of traditional African style.

Chiffon-covered mudcloth at the midriff and bust. Badgley and Mischka probably never imagined their dress (modified Vogue 1806) in this fabric combination!

MUDCLOTH AND CHIFFON DRESSES

Take a piece of mudcloth, add some chiffon, and what do you get? A beautiful dress. I agree that it is hard to imagine, but placing chiffon over mudcloth eliminates its visual ruggedness and softens its look—and the mudcloth motifs peek through the chiffon, adding interesting detail.

Use mudcloth in areas of your garment where the heavy cloth can provide support, such as the midriff or bust. In the design at left, by high-fashion designers Badgley Mischka, I covered the midriff and bust sections with red silk chiffon. The chiffon tones down the mudcloth but doesn't obscure the white motifs.

Here's another pretty dress in which I covered the mudcloth bodice with matching silk chiffon. The chiffon softens the mudcloth but allows the motif to add detail to the dress. I traced a template off of the mudcloth motif and stenciled triangles over the skirt and bodice with fabric paint in a random design.

Design Insight

● *Think beyond the conventional. Unusual fabric combinations such as mudcloth and chiffon can work!*

SHAWLS AND STOLES

Shawls and stoles are another way to wear mudcloth and add striking detail to your outfit. Do something different with a simple stole: wear it as a belt and secure it with your favorite pin.

Shawls don't need to be plain. I made this one (at right) out of mudcloth remnants and raw silk. The fringe adds excitement, and the cowry shells scattered over the scarf are a nice touch. (I attached the shells to the shawl through their holes; you can purchase this type of shell at bead stores.)

This mudcloth stole doubles as a belt (just fasten it with a pin!).

Design by Brenda Winstead. Model: Karen Dove. Photo by Kim Johnson.

Design by Ronke Luke-Boone. Model: Karen Dove. Photos by Kim Johnson.

Together, fringed raw silk, mudcloth, and cowry shells make an exciting scarf. At top, it is fastened with a pin.

WAIST POUCHES, HANDBAGS, AND TOTE BAGS

A waist pouch can be a fashion statement. You don't need a lot of fabric, they are quick and easy to make, and any color will look great. (See page 123 for instructions on how to make a mudcloth waist pouch.)

Mudcloth can be used to make great handbags, tote bags, and small wallets. Make an entire bag out of mudcloth, or use mudcloth as an accent. In some of these summer bags (shown below right), the mudcloth strip doubles as an accent and pocket!

Models: Karen Dove, Karina El-Halabi, and Lisa Scott. Photo by Kim Johnson.

Waist pouches made out of mudcloth look great with jeans or dress pants.

Photo by Charles Tack.

Mudcloth makes fashionable bags.

Kuba Cloth

Kuba embroideries are among the most stunning and visually exciting fabrics in the world. You need no prior exposure to or knowledge of the cloth to be captivated by its beauty. I first saw Kuba cloth in the early 1990s, and I was fascinated. I am constantly amazed and in awe of the skill of the Kuba people.

Kuba cloth is not new to the United States and Europe. Art historians, anthropologists, museum curators, adventurers, and missionaries have collected and exhibited Kuba cloth in Europe since the sixteenth century (Harvard University has had Kuba cloth in its collections in 1893). With the renewed interest in things African in the late 1980s and early '90s, Kuba cloth has broken beyond this intellectual community and taken hold in the popular consumer market. Of all African fabrics now popular in the West, Kuba cloth—which is elegant, reserved, and sophisticated, yet bold and vibrant—has appealed to the broadest audience. Urban dwellers, Africans, and Africa-lovers naturally fall in love with Kuba cloth, but this stunning cloth resonates beyond this natural audience. Suburban dwellers, "chic" people, upscale interior designers, and other "beautiful" people of all races have embraced Kuba cloth, so much so that Kuba cloth has appeared on the sets of popular TV series such as *Frasier* and *Law & Order*, in print ads, and in upscale home décor magazines like *Elle Décor*.

Kuba cloth has also influenced numerous artists, including Henri Matisse, Pablo Picasso, and Paul Klee. Matisse was so fascinated by the cloth that he kept a large collection and displayed it on his studio walls. The next time you look at these artists' work, look for the influence of Kuba cloth and African design.

AFRICA

Kuba cloth comes from central Africa, in the region known today as the Democratic Republic of Congo (formerly Zaire).

Democratic Republic of Congo

Kuba cloth.

✕ The Secret of Kuba Cloth's Appeal

"To western eyes, the cloths are simultaneously bold and intricate, dramatic and subdued, irregular and ordered, as well as asymmetrical and balanced. In all cases they are visually engaging and full of surprises."

Ann E. Svenson, Textile Curator,
Los Angeles County Museum of Art

Since the first foreigners set their eyes upon Kuba cloth in the 1600s, hundreds of articles and books have been written that try to explain the secret of its appeal. Exhibits have been held in Europe, Asia, and the United States. Cloth has been collected for the permanent collections of Western museums. Westerners have traveled to the Kasai region to study the Kuba and uncover the secret of their art. Yet, so much remains to be understood.

Kuba cloth's appeal is in the rhythm of the design. The Kuba skillfully execute—in a manner that appears so naturally complementary—concepts which are contrary to Westerners. Their motifs are abstract, geometric, and angular. Yet, rather than being hard-edged and optically jarring, squares, rectangles, triangles, lines, chevrons, and other geometric shapes merge together in a soft, fluid, and undulating manner. Motifs change; one flows seamlessly into another and, whether by mistake or intent of the designer, nothing seems out of place. The cloth plays with the optical senses. The expected and unexpected appear: motifs recede and proceed, appear and disappear, and meander across the cloth.

The basic color palette is narrow (black, brown, yellow, orange, red, blue, and purple), but the Kuba are masters at using these colors to produce exciting tone-on-tone textiles with flashes of color.

Kuba cloth is *never* boring. When you look at Kuba cloth, you've just got to wonder: "How'd they do that?"

✕ Making Kuba Cloth

The Kuba make their cloth from raffia. Men, women, and children participate in production, but labor is strictly divided: Males collect raffia leaves, boys prepare the fibers into fine silk-like threads for weaving, and women participate in producing fibers for embroidery.

The Kuba Kingdom

The Kuba Kingdom is a matrilineal society which arose in the seventeenth century. Today, it lies within the Democratic Republic of Congo (formerly Zaire) in central Africa, between the Kasai and Sankuru rivers.

The Kuba are a loose federation of eighteen peoples bound together by common mythology, cultural and linguistic affinities, the institution of kingship, and the same political and ideological structure. Each subgroup is independent in its internal affairs.

Visual art is a part of the tradition of every Kuba sub-clan; they decorate everything. Everyday utensils, such as cups, clothing, baskets, storage boxes, door posts... you name it, everything is game for decoration. But it is for their textile art that the Kuba are world renown.

Steps in Making Kuba Cloth

* *Males collect and prepare the raffia threads.*
* *Men weave the base fabric.*
* *Women soften the base fabric.*
* *Women dye the base cloth (if desired) and embroidery threads.*
* *Women decorate the cloth.*
* *Men stitch together the embroidered pieces and/or hem them.*

Using the raffia threads, men weave the base fabric, called *mbal*, on a simple loom. The Kuba do not join raffia strands to form longer continuous threads; therefore, the size of the base fabric is determined by the size of the raffia leaves. Base textiles are small, as compared to the other fabrics covered in this book, and rarely exceed 1 meter (39").

Close-up of dyed *mbal*.

In a final treatment to make a base cloth similar to linen, women dampen the cloth in cold water, wrap it in pieces of old cloth, and pound it. The cloth is dried and the process is repeated until the desired texture is achieved.

Women decorate the cloth with natural and synthetic dyes. First, the artisan decides whether to leave the base cloth in the natural shade or dye it. She also dyes the embroidery threads. The Kuba's famous red dye is obtained from Tukula wood, black and purple dye from iron dross or clay, blue dye from the indigo plant, white from clay, and yellow from local vegetables. Being resourceful, Kuba women also obtain purple dye from ink and pounded carbon paper. More synthetic dyes of these colors are probably used today than earlier in the twentieth century. The varying shades seen in the finished cloth are obtained by controlling the strength of the dye solution. Sometimes the cloth is dyed in tie-dye patterns; this adds interesting detail to the fabric.

Other Names for Kuba Cloth

Kuba cloth is a catchall term used to refer to many types of cloth from the Kuba region. There are three main types of finished cloth: appliquéd, pieced, and embroidered, or cut-pile. Popular terms for the cut-pile cloth are:

* *Velvets or velours, referring to the cloth's cut-pile, plush finish.*
* *Kuba velours, referring to the cloth's cut-pile, plush finish.*
* *Kasai velvets, referring to the region of Africa where the Kuba live.*
* *Shoowa velvet, referring to the Shoowa people who weave the cloth.*

 Types of Decorations

Kuba women make three kinds of finished cloth:
• Appliquéd
• Pieced
• Embroidered (cut-pile)
Of the three, the embroidered cloth is the most sumptuous, dazzling, and prestigious.

Appliquéd cloth.

APPLIQUÉD CLOTH

As the name suggests, the women cover the entire cloth with appliqués of matching or contrasting raffia, which can be round, linear, "L"-shaped, or "comma-" shaped, that are secured with a whip or buttonhole stitch. The decorator positions appliqués at her discretion or for more practical reasons, such as covering up holes in the cloth. Hence, the design of an appliquéd cloth is never complete, for future tears will be covered with appliqués.

PIECED CLOTH

Pieces can be joined in a patchwork pattern or in linear strips. With patchwork designs, small squares of dyed and undyed raffia are joined together in an alternating sequence. The squares may be further embellished with embroidery, making a more dramatic cloth. With the linear pieces, strips of alternating raffia pieces are joined lengthwise.

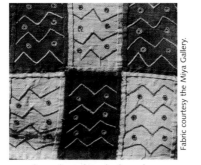

Patchwork Kuba cloth with embroidery on each panel and tie-dyed side panels.

Fabric courtesy the Miya Gallery.

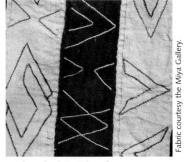

Kuba cloth made of embroidered strips stitched together into a linear cloth.

Fabric courtesy the Miya Gallery.

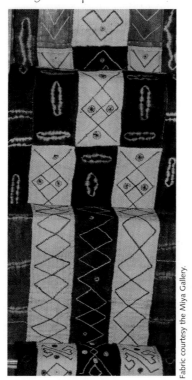

A variety of patchwork cloths at the Miya Gallery.

Fabric courtesy the Miya Gallery.

Patchwork, appliquéd cloth.

Fabric courtesy the Miya Gallery.

Embroidered cloth.

Embroidered cloth.

Embroidered cloth.

Close-up of flat embroidery.

EMBROIDERED CLOTH

These are the most complex and stunning of the Kuba's textiles. In the opinion of many collectors, Shoowa women make the best embroideries, because theirs have the most complex and visually stimulating use of both flat and cut-pile stitches.

Kuba women use two basic embroidery stitches: flat (including the chain, buttonhole, and stem stitches) and the plush, or cut-pile, stitch.

FLAT STITCHING
i.e. chain stitch, stem stitch, buttonhole stitch

CUT-PILE OR PLUSH STITCHING. Raffia threads pulled and caught between weft and warp threads and cut very short so only 1/16" of thread is visible.

Embroidery stitches.

Close-up of plush, or cut-pile, embroidery.

Using dark or light threads, the embroiderer outlines the motif with flat stitches. She then fills in the shape with plush, or cut-pile, stitching in contrasting colors. To make the plush stitch, the embroiderer twists several strands of raffia thread together, threads them through an iron needle, catches a weft thread on the base cloth, and pulls the embroidery threads through until only

Front view of cut-pile embroidery.

Rear view of cut-pile embroidery. Notice that no threads are visible.

1/16" of thread is visible. Using a flat knife, she then cuts the embroidery thread to the same length on the other side of the weft, creating an even tuft of fibers that is held in place without a knot but by the tightness of the weave in the base cloth! No plush embroidery is visible on the back side of the cloth. Periodically, the embroiderer brushes the knife over the cut ends to give the cloth the fuzzy, pile look.

The embroiderer rarely plans her designs at the outset, and she *does not* sketch her design on the cloth in advance; the design develops as she works. Women can take months or even years to complete a single cloth, depending on its size and complexity.

OTHER DECORATIVE TECHNIQUES

The Kuba may add beads and cowry shells to further decorate their cloth, or they may add pom-poms on the edges of the cloth. These are simply attached with raffia fiber.

Close-up of pom-poms at the edge of a piece of Kuba cloth.

Close-up of cloth embellished with beads and cowry shells.

FINISHING THE CLOTH

Men hem the decorated cloth with a running stitch or fringed edge. To make larger pieces used for skirts, they stitch together sections to the desired length before hemming.

Cloth hemmed with a running stitch.

Cloth finished with a fringed edge.

Traditional Uses for Kuba Cloth

The Kuba use cloth for clothing (dance skirts), floor and stool coverings, death shrouds (especially for court burials), to pay tribute, dowries, and, in earlier times, as currency.

Where to Buy Kuba Cloth

* *Specialty (independent) fabric stores*
* *Bead stores*
* *Specialty galleries*
* *Museum shops*
* *Cultural festivals*
* *Mail-order sources*
* *Internet sites*

Kuba Speak

* *Skirts are the long pieces of cloth; they are usually appliquéd but may also be embroidered or a combination of embroidery and appliqué.*
* *Velvets are embroidered, or cut-pile, cloth.*

X Meaning in the Cloth

The Kuba have a vast vocabulary of motifs that depict things from nature, reduced in a stylized, geometric format. There are three categories of design names:
· Patterns that honor famous people or inventors.
· Patterns that refer to parts of an object (i.e. a crocodile's back).
· Patterns that refer to the activity of an object (i.e. a flash for a flash of lightning).

Some motifs and their names are shown on the opposite page. Look for them when you shop.

X Where to Buy Kuba Cloth

Don't expect to buy Kuba cloth at large fabric chain stores—it's highly unlikely they will carry it. Instead, look to specialty (independent) fabric stores, bead stores, specialty galleries, and stores that carry African and ethnic artifacts (i.e. museum shops) throughout the United States and Europe. Cultural festivals are also a good source of Kuba cloth. Mail-order sources for African fabrics may also carry Kuba cloth. On the Internet, do a key-word search for Kuba cloth to find vendors, or bid on auction sites like ebay. Buying Kuba cloth from mail-order or Internet sources has one major drawback: you can't inspect the cloth closely before you buy. Make sure you can return any pieces you are not satisfied with.

X Buying Kuba Cloth: What to Look for

When you are ready to buy Kuba cloth, first learn Kuba speak. If you say to a vendor "I'm looking for Kuba cloth," he or she will probably answer "Skirts or velvets?" Skirts are the long appliquéd or pieced cloths, which are typically rectangular. Velvets are the embroidered pieces, which are often small ("square-ish") pieces, but can also be large and rectangular-shaped.

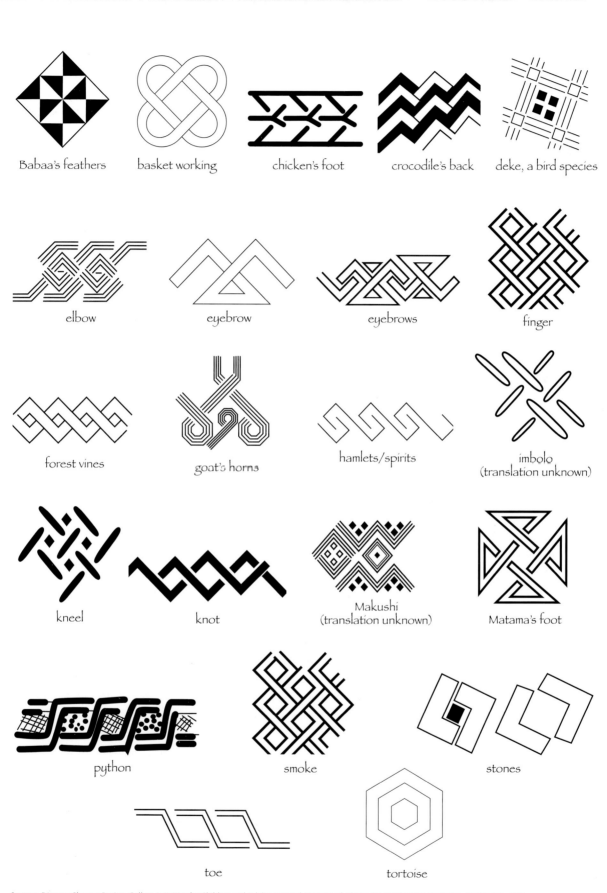

Babaa's feathers

basket working

chicken's foot

crocodile's back

deke, a bird species

elbow

eyebrow

eyebrows

finger

forest vines

goat's horns

hamlets/spirits

imbolo
(translation unknown)

kneel

knot

Makushi
(translation unknown)

Matama's foot

python

smoke

stones

toe

tortoise

Sources: *Discover Shoowa Design, Gallery Activities for Children and Adults*, National Museum of African Art, Smithsonian Institution, Washington, D.C.
The Role of Woven and Embroidered Textiles of the Bakuba: Visual and Historical Dimensions, Wendy Anne Thomas, New York, 1983.

 Buying Kuba Cloth

Now that you know where to buy and the lingo, here's what to look for:
- Buy cloth that appeals to you.
- Consider how shape affects your project.
- Look for good color quality.
- Be aware of holes, creases, and broken stitches.
- Avoid matted cloth.
- Prepare to pay a lot.
- Avoid a strong grass smell.

LOOK FOR CLOTH THAT APPEALS TO YOU

Each piece is unique; you'll probably never find another piece with the exact same color, design, and size. So, if you find a special piece you like (and can afford it), buy it (see the next page for more on price).

LOOK AT THE SHAPE OF THE CLOTH

Kuba cloth is typically "square-ish" and "rectangular-ish" in shape. I say "-ish" because you'll notice shapes aren't exact. Pieces closest to a true square or rectangle are the easiest to work with. Pieced pieces often curve; this curvature may affect your design options.

LOOK AT THE QUALITY OF THE CLOTH

The color should be good and bold. Even beige and taupe should be strong, not faded. Also, the cloth shouldn't be threadbare.

LOOK FOR HOLES

Antique pieces will probably have holes, and newer pieces might. If the cloth has holes in it, think about whether you can work around them. If they are unavoidable, do what the Kuba do: patch over them with raffia appliqués.

If you cannot tell an antique from a modern cloth, contact an institution with experts such as the Smithsonian Institution for advice (see Resources).

LOOK FOR BROKEN STITCHING

The stitching that holds pieces together may break. This is not necessarily bad because you can position your design around these areas, and you may also be able to stitch the cloth together.

LOOK FOR CREASES

Kuba cloth may be creased during shipping or while at the sales outlet. It may be difficult to remove these creases, so think twice about buying very creased cloth (ironing doesn't always work!). You may be able to work around the creases, depending on the design.

LOOK FOR MATTING

Cut-pile cloth should be fluffy, but it can become matted if poorly stored (i.e. under heavy loads). Matted cloth looks shabby, so use it for practice, but final projects won't look good.

DON'T FAINT AT THE COST

Kuba cloth can be expensive, and the better the cloth, the more you'll pay (determined by size, color, embroidery, and vendor discretion). Retail prices may start as low as $15 for lesser quality pieces and run into the thousands for museum-quality and antique pieces. But high-end cloth is well worth the cost because of the time the artisan spent making it, the pride of ownership, and the appreciation you will have for the complexity of the design.

SMELL

Kuba cloth is made from the raffia plant, and the fabric sometimes smells like grass, with some pieces smelling more strongly than others. Although the cloth can be washed, this may not always help get rid of the smell (see page 39 for more information on cleaning Kuba cloth).

Broken stitching.

Front view of Kuba cloth with a crease in the center.

Before You Cut

* Consider prewashing.
* Lay out all of your pattern pieces and cut on a single layer.
* Make sure you are happy with the motif positions.
* Avoid holes or creases.
* Repair broken stitches, if necessary.

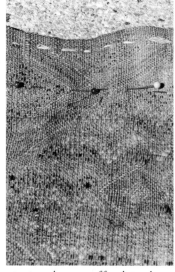

Pinning along a raffia thread.

X Prewash Before You Sew

Consider washing your Kuba cloth before use to remove dirt accumulated during production and shipping (see page 38 for guidance).

X Planning Your Design and Cutting Kuba Cloth

Let the cloth speak to you. Does it suit the project you have in mind? Would it look good in a pillow, as a wall hanging, or as a table runner? Can you incorporate it into a garment?

Do not cut your Kuba cloth if you are not completely sure of your project because you will probably not be able to buy another piece if you mess up. Exquisite embroidery and great design are the reasons you bought the fabric, so let your design reflect this beauty. You don't have to use the entire piece in your project; however, small velvets might only give you one project. Listen to the cloth and your design instinct.

CREASES

As was discussed on the previous page, there are considerations, like creases and holes, you must keep in mind when planning your design. First, look for creases. You might be able to steam creases out by dampening the cloth, holding an iron over it, and applying bursts of steam. Do not place a hot iron on the fabric! Stretch it out, hold it flat with weights, and allow it to dry. Repeat as desired. If you can't remove creases, plan your design around them. Second, avoid purchasing cloth with holes, if possible, or cover them with appliqués that work with your design. (To do this, cut out pieces from unused portions of the cloth and attach them over the holes using a whipstitch.)

"STRAIGHT" FABRIC

Kuba will rarely have a straight selvage like fabric off a bolt. Remember that the pieces are rarely true squares or rectangles; however, Kuba cloth is woven and has warp and weft threads. It's easy to follow a single thread on appliquéd pieces because the threads are easily visible. With embroideries, the threads may not be clearly visible from the right side, so flip the embroidery to the back. Look carefully to discern the crisscross of the weave. Select a thread and follow it down the length of the cloth with pins, as shown on the previous page. Working on the right side, examine how the motif lines up with the pins. Do the pins and motif follow closely? If so, you may be able to straighten your fabric along this pinned thread. If it detracts, you may have to consider cutting along other lines to get the best motif layout.

The top edge is finished with serging and the right edge is finished with a zigzag stitch.

X Sewing Kuba Cloth

At first, you'll probably be a bit nervous about stitching Kuba cloth. You're probably thinking "It's raffia—isn't that a plant? It's exotic. What do I do?" Relax. Yes, raffia is a plant, but so are cotton and linen, and you're not worried about stitching them. Undoubtedly, Kuba cloth is exotic, but therein lies its beauty and appeal. And, with practice, you'll build confidence.

To reduce abrasion as you work, consider underlining Kuba cloth with muslin. For a stiffer hand, use sew-in stabilizer, but eliminate underlining altogether if it gives too stiff a hand for your project.

Your Kuba cloth may stretch a little as you sew (I've experienced it occasionally). If this occurs, trim the seam after stitching.

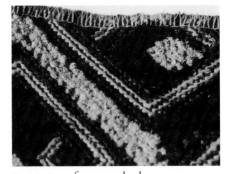

Front view of a serged edge.

Front view of a two-thread overcast serged edge.

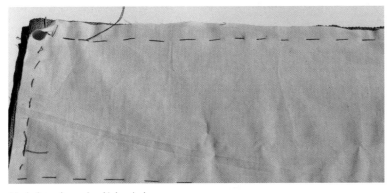

Underlining basted to Kuba cloth.

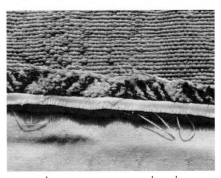

Pressed open seam; notice that the unfinished edge is unraveling.

FINISHING SEAMS

The edges will unravel when they are cut, so you will have to secure them before assembling your project. To reduce unraveling, zigzag or serge the raw edges of cut pieces before assembly. Joined seams can be pressed open, but you'll have bulk at the seams. Account for this in your design.

SEWING KUBA CLOTH TO OTHER FABRICS

You can sew Kuba cloth to many fabrics, including linen, cotton, leather, and suede. I haven't experienced many problems while working with any of these fabrics.

SEWING NOTIONS AND OTHER THINGS

Here are some useful notions and other considerations for sewing Kuba cloth.

- Needle. Universal 70/10, 80/12, 90/14, or 100/16, depending on the fabric's thickness.
- Thread. Cotton-covered polyester for medium-weight fabric, polyester for heavy-weight fabric. Guterman, Molnlycke polyester, and Coats make good products.
- Interfacing. Use sew-in interfacing because Kuba cloth may not withstand the temperatures needed for fusible interfacings (test a corner; if the cloth burns, you know you can't use it!).

X Caring for Kuba Cloth

As was previously stated, Kuba cloth is made from raffia, a natural fiber, and can be washed (and I recommend prewashing it). I have never had problems with washing it, but that is not to say that you will never encounter any difficulties. Remember that Kuba is handmade, and the fabrics and quality vary with each piece. You should be encouraged, though, that Ann Svenson, a textile conservator at the Los Angeles County Museum of Art, has worked with over 200 pieces of Kuba cloth and reports that she has washed, blocked, mended, patched, and mounted cloth with very few problems.

Test your cloth for color fastness before washing by wiping it with a cloth dampened with a solution of detergent. Although I have never had problems with bleeding, it's a good idea to test the detergent before washing. Hand wash Kuba in cold water with a gentle detergent, not in the washing machine (tumbling isn't good for the cloth).

It is not clear how Kuba cloth will stand up to repeated dry cleaning. I know designers who have cleaned Kuba cloth garments and others who dare not. The International Fabricare Institute has no guidance on Kuba cloth, so proceed with caution. If you choose to dry clean it, use a high-quality dry cleaner, one that specializes in antique gowns and fine fabrics. Also, do not dry clean

Kuba Cloth Can Be

- *Hand washed*
- *Dry cleaned (with caution!)*

Kuba cloth very often; limit your designs with Kuba to special occasion articles, or hand wash them, as directed at right.

If you have a rare and/or expensive piece, or you just aren't confident about how to proceed, I advise you to seek advice from either of these sources: the Smithsonian Institution's National Museum of African Art or The Textile Museum in Washington, D.C. (see Resources).

PRESSING

Because you could your burn Kuba cloth by placing a hot iron on it for long periods of time, I recommend using a cotton pressing cloth, which can be purchased at sewing supply stores, to avoid direct contact with the cloth when ironing. During pressing, you may notice a strong grass smell; this should disappear once you remove the iron. You can steam your cloth by holding the iron slightly above the cloth and applying bursts of steam. Treat embroidered cut-pile pieces as you would velvet: use a pressing board for nap, which can also be purchased at sewing supply stores, and use a pressing cloth.

Storing Kuba Cloth

You can store your collection of Kuba cloth in three different ways:
- Flat, in small piles so that the pieces at the bottom don't get matted (important for cut-pile embroideries).
- Rolled.
- Gently folded over (but to prevent creasing, don't stack large folded pieces too high).

Store Kuba velvets in flat piles to prevent creasing.

Store large pieces gently folded over.

Washing Kuba Cloth

* *Fill the bath or plastic tub with cold water (enough to cover the cloth).*
* *Add a gentle detergent (i.e. Ivory, Woolite, or baby soap). Agitate to dissolve the detergent. (Note: Conservators use Synthrapol, an industrial-strength neutral liquid detergent. I buy it at art supply stores.)*
* *Place the Kuba cloth in the soapy water. Soak for 5 minutes.*
* *Agitate the water several times. You may also gently (I emphasize gently) scrub the fabric with a soft brush. For cut-pile embroidered fabrics, work from the rear side, which is flat.*
* *Drain the water. Repeat the process, if you wish, until your cloth is clean.*
* *Rinse the fabric using cold water to remove any soap residue.*
* *Blot excess water from the cloth with a clean towel.*
* *Dry the cloth flat. You may stretch it and anchor the corners with sewing weights. (Conservators block dry cloth.)*
* *The fibers may shrink as the cloth dries; gently hand-stretch it.*
* *Make sure the cloth is completely dry before working with it.*

X Design Ideas

In the United States and Europe, Kuba cloth is most widely used for home furnishings, pillows, or mounted on wall panels—but it can be used for much more!

SELECTING PATTERNS

Price may limit most of us to using only small sections of Kuba cloth in projects. Further, Kuba cloth cannot withstand frequent washing and cleaning, so consider using it only in special occasion garments. Sleeve cuffs, pockets, and hem edges are great areas to include a Kuba accent in your garment design, but you can also use it in exciting fabric collages or a panel on the back of a garment.

LINING

Depending on the fibers, Kuba can feel rough against the skin, so place cloth in areas with limited skin contact, or line the areas that will be close to skin. Rayon and acetate are good options, but your choice of lining depends on your design. Use coat-weight lining for outerwear, and consider the care method for both Kuba and the other fabric when selecting a lining.

COMBINING KUBA CLOTH WITH OTHER FABRICS

Kuba cloth can be combined with other fabrics that have "texture" and an obvious weave, such as linen, raw silk, hemp, or cotton, but suede and leather also can work. Again, consider the care method for Kuba and the other fabric when planning your design. Linen and raw silk may need to be dry cleaned; it isn't clear how Kuba cloth stands up to repeated dry cleaning, so you may not want to wear this garment often.

SHAWLS

Kuba skirts make great shawls. Your cloth may be too wonderful to cut up, so wearing it as a shawl is a nice way to show it off. Stand in front of a mirror and drape the cloth over your shoulders in a flattering manner, anchor the shawl in place with a pin, and you're ready for a dramatic entrance to any social gathering.

Design Insight

⬙ *A shawl can make a dramatic statement.*

VESTS, TUNICS, AND COATS

If you cannot bear to cut the cloth, think of ways to use the entire panel in a garment. Using Kuba on the back of your garment adds a dramatic surprise. In the linen tunic at right, I used the two pieces of Kuba cloth in a panel that I stitched onto the tunic back. The smaller piece toward the neck is cut from a larger cloth. I used the larger cloth in its entirety. I liked the fringe in this Kuba cloth and kept it as a design detail. To tie in the fringe with the rest of the garment, I made a fringe at the hem of the tunic. The design lines are quite simple—the excitement comes from the Kuba cloth, fringe detail, and frog closures! (See page 111 for instructions on how to make this tunic.)

Design Insight

⬙ *Combine Kuba panels for interesting visual effects.*

Model: Karen Dove.
Photo by Kim Johnson.

For a dramatic effect, wear a Kuba cloth as a shawl.

Design by Ronke Luke-Boone. Model: Lisa Scott.
Photos by Kim Johnson.

The tunic back is a great surface for displaying the Kuba panel.

The front of this tunic, The Tibetan Panel Coat (Folkwear 118), is made out of linen, while the back is cut out of Kuba cloth.

Model: Karen Dove.
Photos by Kim Johnson.

For information on creating and altering patterns, see How to Make Sewing Patterns, by Donald H. McCunn, Design Enterprises of San Francisco, 1996.

Here's a vest in which I cut the entire back out of Kuba cloth and the front out of linen. I also modified the original pattern (Folkwear 118, The Tibetan Panel Coat) to fit my Kuba cloth. The original pattern is for an ankle-length coat, but my panel was long enough for a hip-length vest, so I shortened the pattern pieces to fit my cloth. Make your patterns work for you by adapting them as necessary (for instance, shorten a long tunic into a vest, add or remove buttons, or add or leave off a collar). The colors of the front sections match the colors in the Kuba cloth. I also made a fringe at the front hem to match the fringe at the cloth's hem. The interesting details are the exposed, serged edges of the Kuba cloth. To do this, I stitched the seams together, wrong sides facing, serged them, and pressed the finished seams to one side.

Design Insight

◈ Modify purchased patterns to suit your needs; liberate yourself.
◈ Cut entire pattern sections out of Kuba cloth.

A striking coat made entirely out of a Kuba cloth collage.

Design by Brenda Winstead. Model: Lisa Scott.
Photos by Kim Johnson.

Kuba cloth encourages you to be dramatic. This gorgeous coat is made entirely of Kuba cloth and is an excellent example of skillful use of visual effects. Although the color palette is muted, the drama is created by combining several pieces of Kuba cloth in a fabric collage.

DRESSES AND SUITS

The drama of Kuba cloth was perfect for the stunning neckline of this linen suit. I finished the collar edges with two-thread overcast serging, which gave the collar that unpolished, yet finished, look that I wanted. I found the perfect wood buttons that echo the Kuba design to add the finishing touch.

Handbags are another great way to "wear" and display Kuba cloth. With exquisite cloth, be creative with your bag shapes (I call the handbag at right The Picnic Basket). The ochre, black, and tan Kuba cloth is an unusual color combination, but there it works well with leather.

A Kuba collar adds to the drama of this linen suit (Burda V21878).

Handbag design by Ronke Luke-Boone. Model: Lisa Scott. Photos by Kim Johnson.

Design Insight

❖ *You can downplay Kuba cloth's prominence and still achieve high-fashion style.*

You can achieve a high-fashion look by subtly including Kuba cloth into your design. Where is it here? It's in the underskirt that peeks through the dress' front slit. The honeycomb pattern in the Kuba adds visual interest to a simple front, the colors of the linen and Kuba blend well, and the eye flows easily over the entire front. The traditional garment women wear in West Africa was the inspiration for the idea of an overdress with a skirt, but I translated it into a modern outfit.

Subtle use of Kuba cloth creates a high-fashion design.

Design by Ronke Luke-Boone. Model: Karina El-Halabi. Photos by Kim Johnson.

HANDBAGS

Here's another smart handbag out of Kuba cloth and leather. The sleek, simple lines give the cloth center stage, while the leather adds style and makes the bag durable.

HOME IDEAS

Pillows are a wonderfully simple way to add drama to your living room or bedroom. Kuba velvets are most commonly used to make spectacular pillows that are perfect for a room decorated in a modern or ethnic theme. Velvets are small, and the entire piece can be used in one pillow project. Consider cutting up larger skirts to make pillows if you think the fabric is perfect for your project (see page 128 for instructions on how to make Kuba cloth pillows).

Kuba and leather handbags are both fashionable and practical.

Design by Ronke Luke-Boone. Model: Karina El-Halabi. Photo by Kim Johnson.

Kuba and mudcloth pillows.

Kuba pillow and Korhogo throw.

Design by Ronke Luke-Boone. Photo by Kim Johnson.

Design by Ronke Luke-Boone. Photo by Kim Johnson.

You don't have to sew your Kuba cloth; it makes a wonderful accent mat suitable for any room of your home.

You can display long skirts as wall hangings. To make a wall hanging, mount the Kuba cloth on a wooden frame, stitch a sleeve onto the back of the skirt, or sew loops onto one long edge and slide a rod through the sleeve or loops.

Kuba cloth accent mat.

Design by Ronke Luke-Boone.
Photo by Kim Johnson.

CHAPTER 3

Korhogo Cloth

Korhogo cloth is like a brilliant character actor; it is accomplished, yet always in the shadow of stars. With great character actors, you know their faces, can name their films, but you can't remember their names. So it is with Korhogo cloth, always in the shadow of mudcloth and Kente and lacking the stunning beauty of Kuba cloth; many are familiar with the cloth but can't name it. But Korhogo's simple color scheme (figures applied in a black-brown dye on an off-white, natural fabric) and easily recognizable animal and human motifs create a simple, yet elegant, cloth that will stand the test of time and will enjoy broad appeal for its classic designs.

AFRICA

Korhogo cloth is made by the Senufo people in Korhogo, a town in northern Côte d'Ivoire (Ivory Coast) in West Africa.

Côte d'Ivoire

Korhogo cloth.

✗ Protection from the Spirits: Cloth in Senufo Culture

The Senufo, who make Korhogo cloth, believe powerful supernatural spirits live around them. The spirits can be vengeful or quite helpful, so the Senufo strive to stay in the spirits' good graces. To achieve this, they consult a diviner (a religious person in their community) who interprets what should be done. Often, the action involves commissioning a "fila" garment (*fila* is short for *filafani wii* meaning "painted cloth") which serves as protection. The cloth is decorated with humans, human-like figures, and representations of the stars, sun and moon, chameleons, swallows, snakes, fish, lions, and other animals. These animals hold meaning within Senufo culture and mythology, and artisans may group the figures to convey more complex meanings. The diviner also wishes to stay in the spirits' good graces and commissions cloth to use as wall hangings in shrines.

Hunters are important heroes in Senufo culture. They are respected for providing food, but also for their role in founding new villages, a prominent role in Senufo political and religious society. Hunters wear fila shirts and trousers to express their prestige and also for good luck and as protection while hunting (the fabric blends into the background and camouflages the wearer).

The Senufo also commission special cloth for rites of passage such as funerals and other ceremonies of the Poro society. Men and boys are educated in the traditions and culture of Senufo society through the Poro society. There are similar societies for women.

✗ Making Korhogo Cloth the Traditional Way

Men and women have distinct roles in making Korhogo cloth. Both males and females cultivate the cotton. Women spin locally grown cotton into yarn, which men weave into narrow strips (approximately 4″ wide) of cloth. The narrow strips are stitched together to make larger pieces of cloth of varying sizes. Men decorate the cloth using dyes made by women. The artisan stretches the plain cloth on a flat board. Working with a spatula and without preliminary sketches, he traces designs with a light-brown plant-based dye. The first lines are quite faint, and he reinforces the image with additional tracings. The cloth is then dried in the sun. The entire cloth is immersed in a bath of black, transparent dye, turning the whole cloth black. This second dye is a mordant that makes the first dye and decoration colorfast. The cloth is then washed to remove the black dye from all areas but those where it binds to the figures painted in the first step.

The motifs on older Korhogo cloth fit within each strip and were small compared to today's motifs. Older cloth usually had black motifs on white cloth.

Making Korhogo Cloth: Division of Labor

- *Male and female villagers cultivate cotton.*
- *Women spin cotton into yarn and prepare dye.*
- *Men weave and decorate the cloth.*

Nassouko Coulibaly, a member of UGAN Cooperative, demonstrating cotton spinning at the National Museum of African Art, Smithsonian Institution, August 1998.

"Ginning" the cotton (removing seeds from the cotton bols.)

Straightening the cotton fibers using a bow utensil.

Spinning the cotton bol into yarn using a spindle made of bamboo and clay weight. Mrs. Coulibaly holds the ginned cotton in her outstretched left hand.

Photo by Louise Meyer.

An artisan painting on Korhogo cloth, village of Fakaha in Senufo.

X Making Korhogo Cloth the Contemporary Way

Contemporary Korhogo cloth is made by similar methods used in the traditional process. The difference is the artisan does not immerse the cloth in a dye bath after sketching the figures onto the cloth. Working with a second black dye, the artisan traces over the images on the cloth. This second dye, which appears deep black in the bowl, is transparent when poured and acts as a mordant, sealing the first dye. The artisan sometimes fills in the details of each figure using other tools such as brushes.

The motifs on contemporary Korhogo cloth are also larger than those in older cloth. Senufo artisans also create cloth with rust- and ochre-colored backgrounds, where the artisans fill in the space between the figures with colored dye.

Responding to export and tourist markets, artisans may use commercial black dye and imported fabric instead of local dyes and cotton. The result can be very commercial-looking fabric, without the charm of the local-component cloth; however, commercial dyes withstand washing and dry cleaning better than locally produced vegetable dyes.

Contemporary Korhogo cloth is made for the tourist and export market and has lost much of the meaning and symbolism of the old cloth. Artisans decorate contemporary Korhogo cloth with the same stylized human and animal images used in the old cloth but give little consideration in their choice of figures to Korhogo cloth's use as protective clothing.

The Real McCoy!

You can find factory-made fabric (often from Asia) printed with Korhogo cloth motifs, but don't be fooled. Real Korhogo cloth comes from Côte d'Ivoire.

- *There is nothing "even" or factory-looking about real Korhogo cloth.*
- *It is hand-woven and has an uneven weave. Its texture ranges from smooth to rugged, depending on the yarn.*
- *It consists of narrow strips sewn together.*
- *It is not sold by the yard off a bolt.*

Korhogo cloth.

X Meanings of Designs on Senufo Cloth

The Senufo use figures from their mythology and culture to decorate Korhogo cloth. Many of the motifs have meanings. When motifs are combined, the cloth tells stories. Here are some of the meanings of popular motifs.

Guinea fowl: Feminine beauty

Chicken: Maternity

Goat: Male prowess

Tree: Sacred wood where Poro societies meet

Chameleon: Death

Fish: Life and water

Fish bones: Drought

Lion: Royal power

Hunter: Mysteries of the forest

Swallow: Trust

Crocodile and the Lizard: Male fertility

Sun, moon, and stars: First elements God put in the sky the first day the world was created, according to the Senufo

Snake and the Turtle: Earth

Source: Polakoff, Claire. *Into Indigo.* New York: Anchor Books. 1980.

Korhogo cloth is an integral part of Senufo culture, and children start learning to weave and decorate cloth at an early age. Working on a simple child's loom, under the watchful eye of master weavers and in the company of others, young boys weave small pieces of cloth, which they decorate using simple motifs. They progress to larger looms and decorating larger pieces of cloth as their skills improve.

Girls, who are taught separate from the boys, get their own education in spinning cotton into yarn and making the vegetable dyes from older female villagers.

A young Senufo boy learning to weave.

An example of cloth painted by a child learning the art.

Above: Cloth painted by a child learning the art.

Right: A child's loom with samples of work completed by children.

✗ Where to Buy Korhogo Cloth

Korhogo cloth is often sold alongside mudcloth because they use a similar basic cloth and have a similar look and feel. Look for Korhogo cloth at specialty (independent) fabric stores, bead stores, and specialty galleries, and stores that carry African and ethnic artifacts (i.e. museum shops) throughout the United States and Europe. Cultural festivals are another good source for Korhogo cloth. Mail-order sources for African fabrics may also carry it. On the Internet, do a keyword search for Korhogo cloth to find vendors, or bid on auction sites like ebay. Buying Korhogo cloth from mail-order or Internet sources has one drawback: you may not be able to select your cloth yourself; the vendor selects what he or she thinks you would like! Because each cloth is unique, you may have preferred another piece, so check the vendor's return policies.

✗ Buying Korhogo Cloth: What to Look for

First and foremost, buy cloth that appeals to you, but also look for clean, exact design outlines. Korhogo cloth is similar to mud-cloth in how it is made, so look for many of the same qualities:
• Check for rippling and curving.
• Examine the color quality and overall aesthetic of the fabric.
• Pay attention to the positions and repeats of the painted motifs.
• Buy enough cloth!

RIPPLING AND CURVING

I have not encountered rippled, distorted Korhogo cloth as often as distorted mudcloth; however, this can occur if the cloth is unevenly stretched on the board for decorating. (See page 13 for more information on rippling and curving.)

QUALITY AND AESTHETICS OF THE CLOTH

Korhogo cloth has an obvious weave, looks similar to raw silk, and is medium-weight. These qualities are important to note when shopping for real handmade cloth because manufactured Korhogo cloth is becoming common.

Buying Korhogo in Africa

If you are in Côte d'Ivoire's capital, Abidjan, you can find Korhogo cloth at local markets. If you have time, travel north to Korhogo. Local artisans are used to tourists and have cloth ready for purchase. You may also be lucky to witness the cloth being made. One local cooperative headquartered in Korhogo is UGAN (Union des Groupements à Vocation Coopérative d'Artisans du Nord). It has more than 300 highly skilled members including Korhogo textile artisans. UGAN has a beautiful visitor center and gift store. If you have time, commission your own cloth from local artisans (see Resources).

Where to Buy Korhogo Cloth

* *Specialty (independent) fabric stores*
* *Bead stores*
* *Specialty galleries*
* *Museum shops*
* *Cultural festivals*
* *Mail-order sources*
* *Internet sites*

Examine the quality of the painted designs. Cloth dyed with vegetable-based dyes has a deep brown-black color, not the jet black of commercial dyes; however, you may prefer the distinct color commercial dyes provide. Clean, non-blurring lines are more desirable than smudged ones.

REPEATS IN THE DESIGN

The designs on Korhogo cloth rarely repeat evenly. The artisan positions the motifs where he wishes. When you buy, look at how the overall composition appeals to you.

POSITIONS OF THE PAINTED MOTIFS

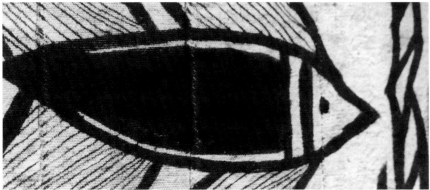

A motif straddles the strips.

Korhogo motifs are large and can straddle two or more strips. These "straddling" motifs will be split if you separate the strips, but your design may require you to cut through these motifs. So, before you buy Korhogo cloth, consider how it will work with your design.

BUYING ENOUGH CLOTH

As with many African fabrics, this is an important consideration. Korhogo cloth is sold in pieces, not by the yard. These pieces are made in a wide range of sizes, the most common being a rectangle approximately 1 yard x 1-1/2 yards, but I have also seen large rectangular pieces (2 yards x 2-1/2 yards), small squares (16" x 16"), and long, narrow rectangles (3 feet x 1 foot). Note: There is nothing hard and fast about these lengths! If your project requires several pieces of Korhogo cloth, always buy extra to allow for positioning motifs (so it is often helpful to choose your design before buying cloth). Finally, expect to pay roughly $15 to $25 for smaller pieces (about 1 yard long) and upwards from $35 for larger pieces (about 1-1/2 to 2 yards long).

X Before You Cut

Korhogo cloth is similar to mudcloth, so before you cut, apply the same considerations as you would for mudcloth; I'll summarize them briefly here (refer to Chapter 1 for details).

X Sewing Korhogo Cloth Without a Walking Foot

Korhogo cloth has a fairly loose weave and sometimes stretches during machine stitching, although the amount of stretching varies with each piece of fabric. If possible, use a walking foot or the dual feed mechanism on your machine. Don't worry if you don't have a walking foot or a dual feed mechanism, because the techniques described below assume you are working with a regular presser foot.

SEWING KORHOGO CLOTH TO OTHER FABRICS

It's easy to prevent stretching and slipping when you are sewing Korhogo cloth to other fabrics (i.e. linen or cotton). Simply put the Korhogo cloth on the underside in contact with the machine's feed dogs. Place the other fabric (cotton or linen) under the presser foot facing you. Stitch. You should have no more slipping. Consider fusing the entire surface of the Korhogo fabric with interfacing (see the guidelines below).

SEWING TWO PIECES OF KORHOGO TOGETHER

Here are some simple solutions when stitching together two layers of Korhogo cloth without a walking foot.
• **The fusible interfacing method.** Fuse the entire surface of Korhogo cloth with interfacing such as Armo weft. This will stabilize the cloth and allow you to sew without the fabric stretching.

If the interfacing or stabilizer gives your fabric too stiff a hand, try these other methods:
• **Fuse narrow strips of lightweight interfacing** (i.e. Armo weft) along the Korhogo cloth's seamline. Stitch the pieces together using an even speed. The interfacing will stabilize the seamline. If you are using sew-in interfacing, follow the guidelines for seam-binding on the next page.

follow the guidelines for seam-binding on the next page.

Before You Cut Korhogo Cloth

* Preshrink the fabric.
* Lay out all of your pattern pieces.
* Secure your strips (if the pattern piece extends over two or more strips).
* Avoid rippled, stretched, and distorted areas.
* Ensure that you're happy with the motif positions.
* Lay out and cut on a single layer as necessary.

Interfacing fused to Korhogo cloth.

Interfacing fused to the seamline.

Korhogo Cloth   53

Seam binding basted to the seamline.

Seam edges finished with serging (above) and zigzag stitching (below).

Caring for
Korhogo Cloth

Korhogo cloth can be:
* *Hand washed*
* *Machine washed*
* *Dry cleaned*
Expect fading and some shrinking with all methods.

• Seam binding, stay tape, or tear-away stabilizer method. First, mark the stitching line on one of the two Korhogo pieces to be sewn together. Second, center the seam binding (or stay tape or tear-away stabilizer) over the seamline you've marked. Sew with the seam binding facing you and the Korhogo cloth against the feed teeth. The seam binding, not Korhogo cloth, will be in contact with the machine's presser foot. You should have no stretching as you sew. Remove tear-away stabilizer after sewing the pieces together.

SEWING NOTIONS AND OTHER THINGS

Here are some useful notions and other considerations for sewing Korhogo cloth.
• Needle. Universal 70/10, 80/12, 90/14, or 100/16, depending on fabric's thickness.
• Thread. Cotton-covered polyester for medium-weight fabric, polyester for heavy-weight fabric.
• Interfacing. Sew-in or fusible interfacing suitable for medium- and heavy-weight fabrics.
• Seam finishing: Zigzag or serging. Finished seams can be pressed open; however, they may be quite bulky depending on the thickness of the Korhogo cloth. Account for this bulk when planning your design.

X Caring for Korhogo Cloth

You can hand wash, machine wash, or dry clean Korhogo. Expect some bleeding with any care method.

When machine washing, use cold water on a gentle cycle with mild detergent (i.e. Ivory) and in a garment bag to reduce abrasion. Remove the cloth from the machine immediately and lay flat to dry. Machine washing tends to cause the dye to bleed quite a bit and may make the off-white sections brown (although this can be a desirable look). Over time, the motifs will fade from deep black-brown or black to a heather brown.

Newly purchased cloth may fade quite significantly with the first dry cleaning from the original color to black-brown or heather brown.

Regardless of what method you use, account for fading as you plan your project, especially garments. Are you going to wear this garment often? If so, can you live with some fading?

If your project combines Korhogo cloth with another fabric, let the care method for the other fabrics guide you (for example, if Korhogo is combined with linen, dry clean the final product).

 Storing Korhogo Cloth

There are no special considerations for storing Korhogo cloth; simply fold up your cloth and store it with your fabric stash.

PRESSING

Korhogo cloth presses very nicely, so you can press as you sew. Lots of steam helps you shape and mold the fabric, but a dry iron can also be used.

X Design Ideas

In the United States, Canada, and Europe, Korhogo cloth is most commonly used for home furnishings. Wall hangings are a popular decoration and pillows are another frequent use. The clothing I see most often are adult and children's vests and coats, which are a great way to incorporate Korhogo cloth into your wardrobe. The design difficulty many encounter with Korhogo cloth is how to incorporate the large animal motifs, in a tasteful way, into a garment. Sometimes you may have to cut up your cloth in order to solve this problem. Here, I show you some designs beyond vests and coats in which Korhogo cloth works wonderfully. Use these ideas as a springboard for your creativity.

SELECTING PATTERNS

As with mudcloth, Korhogo cloth's weight makes it suitable for structured and softly structured clothing, including skirts, coats, jackets, and vests. Select patterns without bulk. Avoid or alter patterns to remove darts. If you can't avoid darts, slash stitched darts and press them open. Replace facings with seam bindings or cut facings out of matching, lighter weight fabrics.

WHICH COMES FIRST: BUYING FABRIC OR SELECTING A PATTERN?

You have to make your design work for Korhogo cloth, so choose a design first. Find a style that makes your Korhogo cloth "shine." This can occur if the cloth adds visual detail to

the design, or if you combine the cloth with another fabric to create interesting contrasts. Sometimes, simple design lines are sufficient to show off Korhogo cloth's motifs.

LINING

Korhogo cloth softens over time; however, depending on the cotton quality, new cloth can feel rough against the skin. Consider lining your garments. The choice of lining depends on the garment and personal preference. Rayon, cotton, and synthetic linings are all suitable. My lining choice depends on the garment I am making.

COMBINING KORHOGO CLOTH WITH OTHER FABRICS

Korhogo cloth combines well with other fabrics with similar visible texture and weight, such as linen, hemp, and wool. Using other fabrics with Korhogo cloth in a design expands your design options because you can use the Korhogo cloth as a design detail that stands out against the other fabric. Consider the care method of your final product when combining Korhogo with other fabrics (see page 54 for more details).

COMBINING KORHOGO CLOTH WITH MUDCLOTH

The basic cottons used to make Korhogo cloth and mudcloth are produced by similar methods, so you can combine the fabrics in one project. I have seen this done in clothing and home furnishings, such as wall hangings. Consider two things if you combine Korhogo and mudcloth. First, are the motifs complementary? Second, is the visual result pleasing? (Taking color, texture, and motifs into consideration.)

COATS, VESTS, AND CASUAL WEAR

Combine Korhogo cloth with heavy outerwear fabrics such as canvas and corduroy to make fashionable coats. Cut the motifs out of Korhogo cloth and appliqué them onto children's clothing such as the back panel on a canvas child's coat.

Vests are another great use for Korhogo cloth. You can use a contrasting cotton, linen, or hemp and make the vest reversible. For reversible winter vests, consider using fleece, flannel, or corduroy for the lining. Think of other features such as a drawstring or elastic at the waistline, and play with fancy button and zipper closures.

Korhogo cloth makes great kids clothing.

Children's coats and vests made out of mudcloth and Korhogo cloth are perfect for fall and winter wear.

Design by Ronke Luke-Boone. Model: Karen Dove. Photo by Kim Johnson.

The Weekend Shift (Hibiscus 1001) made out of Korhogo cloth and linen.

DRESSES AND SUITS

Remember the Weekend Shift (Hibiscus 1001) out of mud-cloth and wool crepe (see page 22)? Take a closer look at the Weekend Shift out of Korhogo and linen. The black trim on the hem is a nice contrast and ties into the black dye of the Korhogo cloth. The figure of the man is still visible on the side panel; however, the other figures in the other two Korhogo sections aren't really discernible but add detail as abstract renderings. It really is okay to cut up your cloth and work it into your overall design!

Design Insight

◈ *Be brave! You can cut your cloth, but you don't have to use the entire piece.*
◈ *Splitting the strips produces abstract motifs that can provide interesting elements to a design.*

Design by Ronke Luke-Boone. Model: Toni Hurd. Photos by Kim Johnson.

Korhogo and linen day-time suit.

Korhogo cloth combines beautifully with hemp in this smart daytime suit. The weight and weave of the fabrics are similar and work well together. There's no reason why backs should be plain. The Korhogo panel on the back of this suit adds a nice surprise to the solid color of the front. Remember this idea when you're looking for ideas for working decorative panels into your garments.

Design Insight

◈ *Korhogo combines beautifully with hemp.*
◈ *Garment backs don't need to be plain.*

I combined Korhogo cloth, mudcloth, and linen in this jacket. The result is a sophisticated, stylish jacket that is suitable for work, casual wear, and special occasions and can be worn over pants, skirts, and dresses. The simple lines, the textures of the Korhogo and mudcloth, and the muted color palette are the secrets to the success of this color-blocked jacket.

Design Insight

◈ *Korhogo and mudcloth are both handspun cotton fabrics. They have the same look and feel and can be combined.*
◈ *Color blocking with a muted, limited color palette can be quite striking. The effect is derived from changes in motifs and subtle color differences rather than sharp color contrasts.*

Design by Ronke Luke-Boone. Model: Karen Dove. Photo by Kim Johnson.

Korhogo cloth, mudcloth, and linen combined in a stylish, modern jacket.

High fashion, raw silk, and Korhogo cloth blend beautifully together in this classic, elegant dress. The simple lines complement the quiet elegance of Korhogo cloth; yet, it adds a dramatic element to an otherwise plain front. A stunning number that will get you noticed in any setting, this dress exemplifies that less is more.

Design by Ronke Luke-Boone. Model: Lisa Scott. Photos by Kim Johnson.

An elegant, yet simple, Korhogo and raw silk dress.

Design Insight

◈ *Korhogo cloth works in high-fashion design.*
◈ *In design, less is more.*
◈ *Korhogo cloth works beautifully with raw silk.*

Courtesy of Louise Meyer.
Photo by Nestor Hernandez.

Korhogo wall hanging in a frame. This cloth is more than 20 years old. The motifs are small compared to today's designs.

Photo by Kim Johnson.

Contemporary Korhogo cloth with large motifs on a decorative rod.

HOME IDEAS

Korhogo cloth is most commonly used for wall hangings; many people mount their cloth on a wooden frame to hang on a wall. If this is your intention, get creative and use a decorative rod from a home furnishing store. The rods with the decorative loops that clip onto the cloth are quite attractive; however, you can also sew loops or a sleeve onto your Korhogo cloth through which you would position your rod for mounting.

Pillows are another common use for Korhogo cloth. To include large motifs, consider making oversized Korhogo pillows to use as floor pillows or accents on your bed (see page 127 for instructions on how to make Korhogo cloth pillows).

Design by Ronke Luke-Boone.

Korhogo and fancy prints pillows.

Placemats are another great idea. Because Korhogo cloth won't withstand frequent washing, try laminating them to make them more durable. (You can purchase laminating products from your fabric or local art supply store.)

You can combine several fabrics when you decorate, as shown in this elegant corner that features a mudcloth framed mirror, Korhogo cloth stand, and Kente cloth wall plaque. The mirror and wall plaque are beyond the scope of this book, but the table is quite easy to make. Cover a sturdy container, such as a box, with thin foam or batting (using glue). Once the glue is dry, cover it with Korhogo cloth.

Design by Louise Meyer.
Photo by Nestor Hernandez.

Laminated Korhogo cloth place mats.

Mudcloth, Kente cloth, and Korhogo cloth are used in this elegant corner.

Photo by Kim Johnson.

CHAPTER 4

Fancy Prints and Wax Prints

Mention African cottons to Americans, and most people will think of fancy prints, those brightly colored, inexpensive African cottons that are everywhere today. Wax prints, fancy prints' more sophisticated "older cousin," are rarely associated immediately with Africa, but without wax prints, there would be no fancy prints.

Today, wax and fancy prints dominate dress in West and Central Africa. African women and men, rich and poor alike, wear fancy prints as everyday wear and wax prints on special occasions. Growing up in Sierra Leone, West Africa, I paid these fabrics no attention, but many years later while in college, I found myself drawn to them again. I was rediscovering the things of my youth, recollecting the wonderful outfits women made out of these distinct cottons. For me, that was the start of a wonderful fashion adventure that continues today. It's amazing to see these cottons combined with silk, satin, linen, and other fabrics and made into fabulous home and personal fashions.

AFRICA

Senegal
Gambia
Guinea
Guinea Bissou
Sierra Leone
Liberia
Côte d'Ivoire
Ghana
Benin
Togo
Nigeria
Gabon
Congo
Cameroon
Central African Republic
Democratic Republic of Congo

Fancy and wax prints are very popular in West and Central Africa.

An array of fancy and wax prints.

X From Wax Prints to Fancy Prints: A Tale of Global Trade

The story of how wax and fancy prints rose to such prominence in Africa is a fascinating tale of colonial times and global trade between Africa, Asia, and Europe.

At the root is the attempt by Dutch colonialists to replicate Javanese batiks and to compete with and undercut local producers in Indonesia with machine-made wax imitations. Unfortunately, early Dutch imitations of Javanese batik weren't very good, and Indonesians rejected the poor Dutch imitations. That story would have ended were it not for the global reach of Dutch colonial power. The Dutch found a market for their imitation batik in the Gold Coast (Ghana today). Locals were familiar with Indonesian batik, which African soldiers, recruited by the Dutch to serve in Indonesia, had brought home. The batik imitations became popular throughout West Africa and, as the market grew, European manufacturers started producing imitation batik specifically for sale in West Africa, adapting the cloth to suit local styles. This cloth is known today as wax prints and is still very popular in Africa.

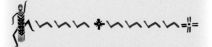

Fancy prints are made in several West African countries, including Benin, Nigeria, and Côte d'Ivoire. Wax prints are made in England and Holland.

From wax prints to fancy prints... A Tale of Global Trade.

In the early 1900s, direct printing technology was developed to make cheaper imitations of the machine-printed wax prints. With this technology, photos could be printed directly on the cloth, which was important for the fabric's success. This cloth is known as fancy prints; it is the inexpensive fabric that is synonymous with African cottons.

After their independence, Africans set up their own textile industries to produce fancy prints for local and regional markets, intending to imitate and compete with European wax producers.

Fancy prints were—and still are—cheap to produce, and the African producers seized market share from their European competitors, driving many out of business. Today, only two European companies (one in England, the other in the Holland) produce fancy prints for the African market.

Fancy prints couldn't completely drive wax prints out of Africa, though. Wax prints are of better quality, more expensive, and had formed roots within communities. These qualities resulted in Africans choosing wax prints for special occasions and more expensive wear over fancy prints even today.

Fancy prints.

Fabric courtesy ABC Wax.

Wax prints.

X Making Wax and Fancy Prints

Unlike the other fabrics discussed in this book, wax and fancy prints are factory-made.

Wax prints are made in a multiple-step, complicated process. In the basic process, using a machine, a thin resin resist is rolled in a repeating pattern onto both sides of the cloth. The resin is left to dry. Once dry, the cloth is carefully crumpled to crack the resist. The cloth is then immersed in a dyebath (usually blue), saturating the cloth with color. A mordant is added to the dyebath; this produces a colorfast cloth that fades slowly. Dye seeps through the cracks in the resin, creating thin veins of color on the cloth known as textile. Other colors are added using color blocks, on which an image is etched and color is applied there. Other types of wax prints are made in more complicated processes (the process used depends on the desired final product).

Fancy prints are made using a roller printing process. A design is cut onto a series of large brass rollers, one for each color. The rollers are attached to a printing machine one after another. The fabric passes under the rollers, and the design is printed on one side, starting with the lightest color and ending with the darkest. The process is simpler and cheaper than that for wax prints.

X Wax and Fancy Prints: How Do You Tell the Difference?

To the untrained eye, wax and fancy prints may appear similar at first glance. Fancy prints, however, are easily distinguishable from wax prints. Fancy prints are printed only on one side, so they have a distinct right and wrong side, while wax prints are printed on both sides and have no distinguishable right or wrong side.

Making Wax Prints

* *Thin resin resist applied to both sides of fabric.*
* *Dry resin is cracked.*
* *Cloth immersed in blue dye bath.*
* *Blue dye seeps through cracks onto fabric.*
* *Additional color added using color blocks.*
* *Both sides are printed.*

Making Fancy Prints

* *Design is cut on brass rollers.*
* *Rollers attached to printing machine.*
* *Fabric is passed under the rollers.*
* *Lightest color printed first, darkest last.*
* *Only one side is printed.*

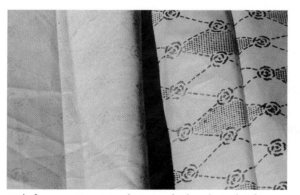

With fancy prints, it is obvious which side is the front and which is the back.

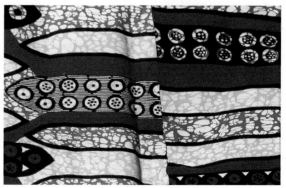

With wax prints, it is difficult to determine which side is the front and which is the back.

Fancy prints with Kente motifs are popular in the United States.

Fancy prints with mudcloth motifs are popular in the United States.

Where to Buy Wax and Fancy Prints

* *Specialty fabric chain stores*
* *Mail order sources*
* *Cultural festivals*
* *Internet sites*

X More Than Cloth

Wax and fancy prints are more than colorful dress in Africa; they are deeply embedded in the social fabric of African society. The designs on many fabrics draw on African proverbs, customs, and aesthetics, but they are also used for social commentary. Fabric names reflect opinions on a wide range of issues, including women's issues, politics, and everyday life. An interesting result is that ordinary people who have limited access to media outlets can express their opinions publicly through the cloth they wear!

Because fancy prints are inexpensive to produce and photographs can easily be reprinted on the cloth, fancy prints provide a canvas for the rich and powerful to project their status. Wealthy families commission fancy prints with family photographs to commemorate special social occasions such as weddings and funerals. Politicians commission fabric in support of their campaigns, and businesses use the cloth to advertise their products.

Many of the fancy prints available on the U.S. market today reflect modern and traditional designs found in Africa. ABC Wax has a vast archive of wax print designs that are based on designs popular in Africa.

X Where to Buy Wax and Fancy Prints

In the United States, specialty (independent) fabric and fabric chain stores carry fancy prints. Wax prints are found in better fabric stores and in specialty stores that cater to expatriate African communities. In Europe, you'll probably find fancy and wax prints at specialty stores. Cultural festivals in the United States and Europe are also good sources for both. Mail-order sources for African fabrics may also carry them. On the Internet, do a keyword search for wax and fancy prints to find vendors, or bid on auction sites like ebay. Buying wax prints from mail-order and Internet sources should present no unique problems, but buying fancy prints from mail-order or Internet sources has one major drawback: you can't inspect the cloth before you buy, so check the return policies of mail-order and Internet vendors. Fancy prints are inexpensive (at an average of $5 per yard), while wax prints cost more (anticipate spending about $12 to $15 per yard).

X The Real McCoy!

Imitation is the greatest form of flattery. Fancy and wax prints are so popular that they are widely copied by textile producers in Asia and sold as "ethnic prints" in fabric stores throughout North America and Europe. If you are a stickler for the real thing, look along the selvage for manufacturing information, including place of origin. Fabric from Africa includes that made by Afriland, Sotiba, and Homeland. African source countries include Ghana, Benin, Senegal, Côte d'Ivoire, and Nigeria. Wax prints are made in Holland and England (the only English producer of wax prints is ABC Wax, A. Brunnschweiler & Company, in Manchester, England).

X Buying Fancy Prints: What to Look for

When you walk by a table piled high with fancy prints, something about the fabrics may captivate you, and you've just got to stop to look. Maybe it's those wonderful, vibrant colors that beckon or the motifs you can't resist. Before you get carried away, here are a few things to remember when you buy fancy prints:

- Make sure the colors suit you (if you are using them for a garment).
- Check for crooked, slanting motifs (make sure they are straight of grain).
- Check fabric for blank patches.
- Check the orientation of motifs.
- Buy enough fabric (dyelots may be irregular).

ARE THOSE YOUR COLORS?

Intense prints and bright colors make fancy prints unique. Those rich reds, vibrant blues, and acid greens offset with gold are all you need to get your imagination going. You dream up great outfits you can make from these fabrics, but wait! Before you buy, think about whether those are your colors. When the colors of fancy prints are right for you, you'll look absolutely stunning in any outfit, but if the colors are wrong, the effect can be disastrous! The moment you walk into a room, everyone will know something's not quite right, even if they can't put their finger on it. What I call the "clown effect" kicks in (a men-

Buying Wax and Fancy Prints in Africa

Buying wax and fancy prints in Africa can be great fun because there's lots of fabric to choose from, the displays are colorful and fun to look at, and you might be able to haggle. Go to any market in any city in West and Central Africa and you'll find fabric vendors. In Nigeria, a popular market is the Balogun market in the capital, Lagos. In Ghana's capital, Accra, make your way to the Makola Market.

Fancy and wax prints are made and sold in Africa in multiples of 6- and 12-yard pieces because 6 yards are the standard amount African women need to make their typical three-piece outfits (consisting of a tailored skirt or wrapper, blouse, and second wrapper). The additional 6 yards in a 12-yard piece can be given as a gift or used for matching children's or men's outfits.

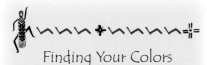

Finding Your Colors

To get a color analysis, look for these books on color and style at your local bookstore or library.

- *Color Me Beautiful by Carole Jackson*
- *Essence Book on Style edited by Patricia Mignon Hinds*
- *Style & You by Clare Revelli*
- *Women of Color by Darlene Mathiss*

Here, the motif veers off the edge.

tal link between intense bright colors and clown clothing). The last thing you want is for people to be reminded of clowns when you're wearing fancy prints—the effect you want is that your natural beauty is enhanced.

So, do you know your colors? Which colors make you look natural? Dramatic? If you can answer these questions, use this knowledge when you buy fancy prints. If you can't, consider getting a color analysis from a cosmetologist after which you can find out which colors suit you. Fabric costs money, and sewing takes time, so it makes sense to make sure that your investment pays off with clothes that make you look good.

ARE THE MOTIFS ON THE STRAIGHT GRAIN?

Slanted, off-grain motifs are a common problem with fancy prints. Somehow during manufacturing, the motifs are printed in such a way that they end up slanting off the lengthwise grain, which causes problems when you're cutting out your pattern.

So, before you buy it, open up the fabric and look at the motif. Is it straight throughout the length or does it slant? Sometimes it is hard to tell whether or not the motifs slant just by looking at the fabric. To be safe, buy extra fabric to get around the sections of slanting motifs when you cut. If it is clearly visible that the motif slants off-grain, negotiate a discount with the store. If this works, think about buying the fabric; a good discount might compensate for the aggravation you could face when sewing. If it doesn't work, don't buy it—why should you pay full price for a shoddy product?

DOES THE FABRIC HAVE BLANK PATCHES?

Periodically, I find fabric with blank patches. These occur when the fabric inadvertently folds during the printing process and sections beneath the folds aren't printed. You may be able to work around the patches, but think before you buy.

HOW ARE THE MOTIFS ORIENTED?

Examine the orientation of the motifs when you buy fancy prints. Often, figures with definitive up and down positions are oriented perpendicular to the selvage instead of running along the lengthwise grain. Here's an example: Let's say a fancy print has a hut motif. The huts should be oriented as shown in the figure on the left. If you draw an imaginary line through the roofs, it will be parallel to the selvage. Often, however, I find fabric with the motifs oriented in other ways. For example, the huts in the figure on the right are at a 90° angle to the selvage, and the hut run parallel to the crosswise grain. You would have to lay your pattern along the crosswise grain to cut this fabric in order to have the huts oriented correctly.

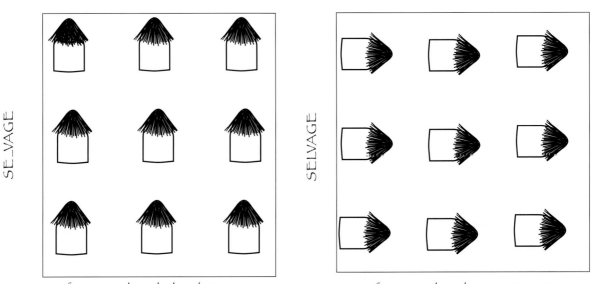

Motifs running along the lengthwise grain.

Motifs running along the crosswise grain.

INCONSISTENT DYELOTS

Inconsistent dyelots are common with fancy prints. You may find variations in the shades of a color in the same fabric from different batches. This can present problems if you run out of fabric and cannot find a match in a store. To be safe, buy all of your fabric from the same piece or bolt.

These two pieces of fabric have the same pattern but came from a different dyelot.

X Buying Wax Prints: What to Look for

Wax prints do not present the problems of fancy prints because their color palette is more muted and sophisticated. But, you still need to know what colors suit you, so once you find colors and designs you like, the only remaining issue is to determine how much fabric to buy.

X Preshrinking Before You Sew

Preshrinking is recommended for most fabrics, and I recommend preshrinking fancy and wax prints (see pages 74 and 75 for care instructions).

X Preparing to Cut Fancy Prints

Most of the remaining challenge with fancy prints comes with cutting.

HOW TIRED ARE YOU?

Whatever you do, **do not** cut fancy prints when you are tired or rushed. Successful garments start with preparation and layout, and layout is really a mental process. The very detailed motifs and intensity of fancy prints present challenges. They demand a similar level of mental engagement as plaids and checks, but with fancy prints, additional bright colors and busy motifs can tax your mind and mood, forcing silly mistakes.

DO YOU HAVE ENOUGH FABRIC?

Earlier, we talked about buying extra fabric to get around slanting motifs and inconsistent dyelots, but here's one more reason to buy extra fabric: you'll need it to match motifs so that you have no visual breaks in your finished garment.

CHECK FOR AND LINE UP REPEATS

When laying out pattern pieces on fancy prints, think ahead to the finished garment and how the motifs will line up in "criti-

When You Cut Fancy Prints

* Be alert.
* Make sure you have enough fabric.
* Check for repeats in the motif.
* Line up repeats before you cut.
* Cut on a single layer to match motifs.

cal areas" such as front openings, patch pockets, and sleeves. The techniques for cutting plaids or checks are applicable here. **Cut your pattern on a single layer of fabric.** Check for a repeat in your fancy print. Is it regular or irregular? Take this into account when cutting. (For more information on sewing plaids and checks, see *The Experts' Book of Sewing Tips & Techniques*, Rodale Press, 1995.)

• **Tracing Trick.** Here's a tip you can use to make sure that your motif lines up correctly when you're cutting a pattern piece that calls for "Cut 2 of fabric." I'll describe the technique using the bodice front shown at right. Trace outlines of key features of the motif onto the bodice front. Pay attention to tracing enough motifs at important construction areas (for example, the seamlines, front closure, and center line). Cut out one side of the pattern (remember you are cutting on a single layer of fabric). Flip the pattern over to cut out the other bodice front. Match the motifs traced on the pattern tissue with similar motifs on the fabric. Secure pattern pieces with pins or weights and cut out the other bodice front. If done correctly, this method will produce foolproof results.

• **Disappearing pockets.** When a design calls for patch pockets (those pockets that are stitched flat onto the outer pieces of a garment, including a jacket, skirt, or trousers), and you're work-

ing with a fabric with a motif, it's a sign of good craftsmanship if the pockets "disappear" into the garment (look at expensive clothes and you'll see what I mean). Whether it's plaids, checks, or fancy print motifs, you don't want any visual interruption at the pockets (like the example on the left). The transition should be seamless (like the example on the right). To do this, I use the tracing trick described above.

Tracing the motif on your pattern makes cutting easier.

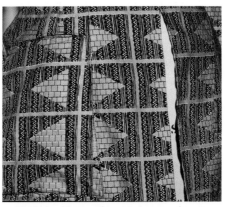

Pocket detail on a fancy prints jacket. This motif veered off the straight grain quite significantly, so lining up the pocket and jacket motifs was challenging. I decided that matching motifs horizontally was more important than the vertical lines. As you can see, the horizontal lines match quite well, while the slight offset is not readily visible. If you choose to add pockets to a garment, you may have to do this as you work with fancy prints.

Fancy prints jacket; here, the motifs are aligned properly.

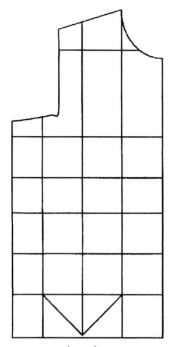

Correct pocket placement;
pockets "disappear."

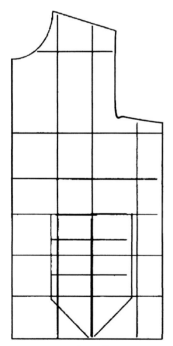

Incorrect pocket placement;
pockets don't line up.

Here's what you need to do: Find the pattern piece that has front pockets (i.e. jacket front). On the jacket front pattern tissue, trace the motifs around the pocket placement positions. Next, get the pocket pattern. Mark the seam allowance all around the pocket pattern piece. Place this seamline over the pocket placement line on the jacket front pattern piece. Make sure that you match the seamline (not the outer edge of the pocket pattern piece) to the pocket placement lines on the jacket front. Trace the motifs onto the pocket piece. When cutting the pocket piece out of fancy prints, match the traced motifs with matching motifs on the fabric. Now you're ready to cut.

• **Set-in sleeves.** When cutting set-in sleeves, use the same techniques as for plaids and checks. Match the motif at the underarms and then check it at the front and back sleeve notches. Does the motif line up with the notches on the garment pieces where the sleeves will set in? Adjust until you are satisfied with the match, then cut.

• **Slanting Motifs.** Many pattern pieces need to be cut on the lengthwise grain. If all is right with your fancy print, the motifs will also run parallel to the selvage, and all will be well with your garment. But fancy prints aren't perfect. Remember our earlier discussion about veering motifs? Cutting is where this comes into play. As you lay out your pattern pieces, be alert as to where the motif veers off the grain. Lay your pattern pieces around these sections. And don't be shocked if you waste a lot of fabric!

Preparing to Cut Wax Prints

Follow the guidelines for fancy prints for lining up repeats (see page 70). Color issues, inconsistent dyelots, and slanting motifs applicable to fancy prints aren't relevant here.

Sewing Fancy and Wax Prints

Fancy and wax prints are both light- to medium-weight cotton and stitch easily, although wax prints are softer and stitch easier, particularly around curves, than fancy prints (which can be fairly stiff and difficult to work around curved seamlines). Preshrinking helps soften fabric for sewing.

Set your machine to suit the weight of the fabric. Most often, this will be for a medium-weight fabric.

SEWING WAX AND FANCY PRINTS TO OTHER FABRICS

Wax and fancy prints are factory-produced cottons. You should have no difficulty stitching them to other fabrics, such as linen, satin, and hemp.

FINISHING SEAMS

Trim away any excess fabric. Serge, pink, zigzag, or cover raw edges with bias tape. Joined seams can be pressed open.

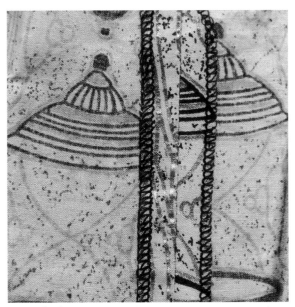

Serged edges.

Pinked edges.

Bias-covered edges.

SEWING NOTIONS AND OTHER THINGS

Here are some useful notions and other considerations for sewing fancy and wax prints.
• Needle. For either fancy or wax prints, use a universal size 65/9, 70/10, or 80/12, depending on the fabric's thickness.
• Thread. Use cotton-covered polyester thread.
• Interfacing. Use sew-in or fusible interfacing, depending on the desired hand.

X Caring for Fancy Prints

The rules for caring for fancy prints are simple: wash them in cold water and **do not** dry clean fancy prints with gold coloring!

Hand washing or gentle washing in your machine is recommended for fancy prints. If you choose machine washing, use cold water, on the gentle cycle with mild detergent (i.e. Ivory) in a garment bag (if the print has gold highlights). The garment bag reduces abrasion and protects the fabric's shine.

Fancy prints fade with washing; account for this as you plan your design. Are you going to wash the garment often? If so, can you live with some fading? In my experience, fading has never been excessive, and my clothes don't look washed out. If faded garments bother you, though, use fancy prints to make special occasion garments that you won't wear often.

Line-dry fancy prints or use the clothes dryer. If using a dryer, use a garment bag to reduce abrasion and remove the fabric immediately when dry to reduce crumpling.

Frequent washing and drying fancy prints can leave a garment limp. The simplest remedy is to press slightly damp, limp garments with lots of spray starch and steam.

Dry cleaning strips away the gold shine on shiny fancy prints, leaving dull sections throughout the fabric where the gold once was. Fancy prints stripped of their gold are "poor cousins" to gleaming fabrics.

There are two ways of protecting and restoring the shine whether dry cleaning or washing: Either you can paint over the shiny sections on your fancy print with gold fabric paint after you cut out the pattern pieces as a precautionary measure, or you can paint over sections on your finished garment as they fade from normal wash and wear. Regardless, make sure that the fabric paint is washable and can be ironed (test a swatch of fabric first).

Caring for Wax and Fancy Prints

* Fancy prints can be machine and hand washed. Do not dry clean!
* Wax prints can be washed or dry cleaned.

The fabric on the left was washed in cold water, and the fabric on the right was dry cleaned.

✕ Caring for Wax Prints

You can hand wash, machine wash, or dry clean wax prints. If hand or machine washing, use cold or warm water. There's no need to use a garment bag when washing wax prints. The fading with washing and dry cleaning should be minimal, but if you are concerned, test swatches.

STORING

There is nothing special to note about storing wax and fancy prints. Simply fold and add them to your fabric stash.

PRESSING

Wax and fancy prints are cottons and press easily. Set your iron to the appropriate temperature for cotton, and you're ready to go.

✕ Design Ideas

Fancy and wax prints are the most accessible of all of the fabrics covered in this book (and fancy prints are the least expensive). They are bright, colorful, and wonderful for adult and children's clothes (including men's summer shirts), accessories, and home furnishings.

SELECTING PATTERNS

Both fabrics work well for lots of styles, including A-line styles, full-gathered skirts, shift dresses, and jackets. You can cut fancy prints and wax prints on the bias, but you won't get the elegant drape you get with soft fabrics (although you could get an interesting visual effect, depending on the motif).

Fancy prints can be fairly stiff cotton and can be difficult to work around curved seams such as princess seams. If you are a beginning sewer, avoid princess seams when working with fancy prints.

BALANCING FANCY PRINTS WITH OTHER FABRICS

Fancy prints are bright, intense, and often very busy—sometimes that's too much color and detail to take at one time. Tone down fancy prints by combining them with another fabric in a solid color, one color in the fancy print you like. I combine fancy prints with linen, silk, and satin to make fashionable casual, work, and special occasion clothes.

COMBINING WAX PRINTS WITH OTHER FABRICS

Wax prints have muted colors, but you can still consider combining them with another fabric in a matching solid color.

Design by Ronke Luke-Boone.
Photo by Kim Johnson.

SLEEPWEAR

Start your day in a bright cotton wax prints robe. This one is trimmed with contrasting red floral cotton and is wonderful in the spring and summer. Men and children may also love a bright, cheerful cotton robe for hot weather months.

Morning robe made out of wax prints and contrasting cotton.

DRESSES AND JACKETS

For casual daytime outfits, think of combining fancy prints with cotton, linen, or hemp. This two-piece outfit has a fancy print jacket over a linen dress. The gold-yellow linen picks up the gold tones in the fancy print. The blue fancy print has a diamond motif that runs through it. To tie the dress and jacket together, I embroidered blue diamonds around the neckline of the dress, and hemmed it using a satin stitch. The result is a smart outfit suitable for work or play.

Model: Lisa Scott.
Photo by Ken Hong.

The fancy prints' motif inspired the embroidery at the neckline of the linen dress.

Design Insight

❖ *Your designs should have simple lines.*
❖ *Detailed fancy prints pair well with a single-color fabric.*

Here's a pretty summer wax print dress. Clean, simple lines complement the sea creature motif.

Design Insight

❖ *Simple can be stylish.*
❖ *The focus is on the fabric.*

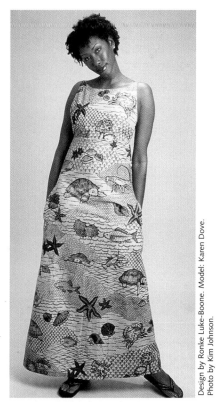

Design by Ronke Luke-Boone. Model: Karen Dove.
Photo by Kim Johnson.

Simple, clean lines make this a classic dress.

This very stylish jacket is a collage of fancy prints, manufactured mudcloth, silk tweed, and ultra suede. The fabrics are coordinated and pieced into a casual jacket. The secret to the success of this piecing is maintaining the red tones throughout the entire garment (the other colors harmonize well with red).

Piecing and collaging are great ways to use your remnant fabrics. Quilters are familiar with color coordination and piecing; non-quilters need not be daunted. With a little practice, you'll be piecing too! Look through your remnants for fabrics that look good together. Lay them side by side and play with the combinations until you're happy with the results. Use a product like HTC's Quilt Fuse to help you with piecing (on which you can position your fabric pieces where you want them and fuse them in place with a hot iron).

Fancy prints pieced with silk tweed, ultra suede, and manufactured mudcloth look great in a contemporary jacket.

Design by Lisa Shepard. Model: Karina El-Halabi. Photos by Kim Johnson.

Design Insight

◈ *Piecing creates wonderful visual contrast.*

Model: Karen Dove.
Photo by Kim Johnson.

Folkwear Pattern's Chinese Jacket pieced in fancy prints and linen.

I made this fancy prints and linen jacket out of remnant fabrics using Folkwear Pattern's Chinese Jacket. I cut the jacket front into smaller sections and pieced the fancy prints and linen together in a way I liked. It's quite easy to do. The jacket can be dressed up with smart pants or worn with jeans for a casual look (see page 114 for information on how to make this jacket).

For a dramatic special occasion look, combine fancy prints with dupioni silk or satin. The shine of dupioni silk, satin, and fancy prints complement each other, while the stiffness of dupioni silk and fancy prints also works well together.

This delicate, peachy-pink fancy print matched the bronze dupioni silk perfectly. Care requirements for the two influenced my design. Dupioni silk needs to be dry cleaned to retain its shine, and fancy prints need to be washed to retain their shine (dry cleaning will strip the gold from the fabric), so I created a two-piece design, a full skirt with a simple blouse. The result, what I call my prom dress, is simple, yet very elegant.

Model: Lisa Scott.
Photo by John Rusnak.

The shine of fancy prints and dupioni silk complement each other.

Design Insight

◈ *Fancy prints combine with dupioni silk for a stunning evening look.*
◈ *You can achieve high fashion with simple style lines.*
◈ *The care method requirements should influence your design.*

Model: Lisa Scott.
Photo by Kim Johnson.

The wax print is the focus of this design.

Saris, where endless lengths of beautiful cloth envelop a woman's body, have always fascinated me. Inspired by the sari, I combined a cropped dupioni silk blouse with a full fancy prints skirt to make this adorable outfit at right. The beaded fringe adds another hint of the exotic to a very modern outfit.

The wax print at left is so dramatic that all I needed was a simple sheath dress design to give the fabric center stage.

Model: Lisa Scott.
Photo by John Rusnak.

The fancy prints skirt and dupioni silk blouse combine together in a stylish cocktail outfit.

Design Insight

◈ *The fabric is the focus.*
◈ *Simple design lines are best.*

A Badgley Mischka design in fancy prints and hand-stenciled satin (modified Vogue 1806).

Here's another wonderful ensemble that highlights the drama of fancy prints. I doubt Badgley and Mischka ever anticipated seeing their design (Vogue 1806) in fancy prints, but here is a sophisticated dress. Topped with a fancy prints jacket, this dress would be perfect for an elegant event.

I loved the colors and pattern of this fancy print (black and brown checks within a gold grid), so I quilted the jacket using black thread in a diagonal pattern, creating another grid at a 45° angle to the gold grid in the fabric. The interplay between the two grids adds interesting detail to the fabric.

I didn't want to make the entire dress out of fancy prints, so I used a satin that picked up the gold. I then made templates of the fancy prints' check pattern and a portion of its gold grid. Using black and bronze fabric paints, I stenciled checks and grid portions randomly over the skirt and bodice sections of the dress and blouse. The stenciling ties the satin into the fancy print.

Quilted jacket made out of fancy prints.

Design Insight

◈ *Fancy prints combine well with satin.*

◈ *A little fabric goes a long way when skillfully combined with other textiles.*

◈ *The motifs on fancy prints are great sources of design ideas for stenciling and stamping.*

◈ *Surface design, such as stenciling and stamping, open up many more creative avenues.*

I used the same stenciling idea in the party dress at right. This is the same design as the Summer Sassy Number shown in mudcloth and linen (on page 23), but this time I interpreted it in fancy prints and hand-stenciled satin. The sweeping seamlines pull your eye through the whole garment as they do in the mudcloth version; however, the visual contrast is sharper in this dress because of the changing textures and colors between the fabrics. When you interpret your designs in different fabrics, you'll learn how a design can be made to look different.

In the stunning outfits below, I expressed modern, high-fashion interpretations of basic design styles common in West African women's attire. It is common for African women to layer garments, for example a blouse over a long wrapper, a caftan-style robe over another dress, or a wrapper tied over the bust; those are the basic pieces of these outfits. The overdress can be worn over a simple sheath or a long skirt, but it all depends on how daring one is.

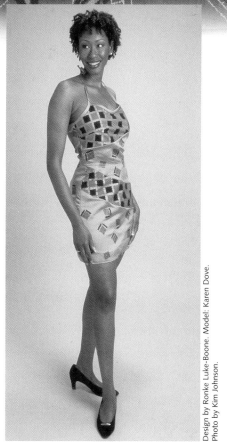

Design by Ronke Luke-Boone. Model: Karen Dove.
Photo by Kim Johnson.

Summer Sassy Number in fancy prints and hand-stenciled satin.

High-fashion style inspired by the lines of West African women's wear.

Design by Ronke Luke-Boone. Model: Lisa Scott.
Photos by John Rusnak.

Fancy Prints and Wax Prints 81

I chose fancy prints and dupioni silk for this outfit. The shine of both fabrics complemented the dramatic look I wanted. The overdress is a green and gold fancy print lined with yellow-gold dupioni silk. The sheath dress and skirt are made out of yellow-gold pleated dupioni silk—a stunning number!

Modern style for modern lives.

Design Insight

◈ *Fancy prints combine well with dupioni silk.*
◈ *The style lines of traditional garments are a great source of ideas.*
◈ *Fabrics can turn simple design lines into a dramatic garment.*

Design by Ronke Luke-Boome. Model: Karen Dove. Photos by Kim Johnson.

ACCESSORIES

Hats and hair bows made from fancy prints are great accessories. The are easy to make and add colorful detail to any female's hair—especially girls. (See page 125 for information on how to make hair bows.)

Cool hats made out of fancy prints and mudcloth.

Photo by Kim Johnson.

Pretty cotton print and Kente cloth hair bows.

MEN'S SHIRTS

Casual men's shirts out of fancy prints look smart at a summer barbecue or the beach. Think of them as the African version of a Hawaiian shirt: bright, colorful, and just right for summer fun!

Casual men's shirts made out of fancy prints.

Model: Duane Pergerson.
Photos by Kim Johnson.

CHILDREN'S CLOTHES

Fancy prints make wonderful children's clothes. The vibrant colors and motifs are perfect for adorable children's outfits. Here are some spring and summer dresses and shirts in which kids look wonderful.

Kids look cute in vibrant fancy prints.

HOME IDEAS

You can have lots of fun brightening up your home with wax and fancy prints. Here are a few ideas, but the possibilities are endless! (You might want to try drapes, pillows, shower curtains...)

Cook with a touch of Africa. An apron, oven mitt, and potholder made of fancy prints are simple accents that would make a dramatic statement in your kitchen (see pages 132-134 for instructions on how to make this ensemble.) They are simple to make, and the cotton will withstand repeated washing.

Place settings are an easy accent for your dining area. These cheerful mats are a bright start to your day. Consider using fancy prints to make table mats for special occasions and holidays such as Thanksgiving, Christmas, and Kwanzaa (see page 131 for instructions on how to make placemats).

Photo by Kim Johnson.

An apron and oven mitts made out of fancy prints add a colorful touch of Africa to your kitchen.

Fancy prints place mats add color to a dining table.

Kente Cloth

Kente cloth is made by the Ashanti people of Ghana and the Ewe (pronounced Ev-eh) people of Ghana and Togo. Today, it is probably the most widely known African fabric in the world. Unlike other African fabrics, which are primarily used and known for their aesthetic qualities, Kente cloth is associated with enormous symbolism. Starting in the 1960s, and particularly in the '90s, African Americans, Africans, and blacks around the world have used Kente cloth to express cultural heritage, pride, achievement, and ties to Africa. These strong socio-political associations have anchored Kente as the dominant fabric and symbol in global black culture, but have limited its use by non-blacks, unlike mudcloth or Kuba cloth; because blacks have so strongly identified with it, others feel that they don't have "permission" to use Kente cloth.

AFRICA

Ghana and Togo lie in West Africa.

Ghana   Togo

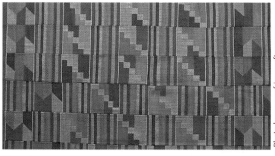

Ewe Kente.

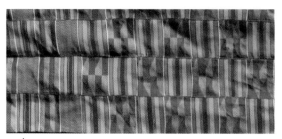

Ashanti Kente.

Photo by www.africancrafts.com

✗ Real Kente

Today, many fabrics—including printed cottons and rayons, woven fabrics, and strip woven cloth—are sold as Kente. Are they all Kente? Yes and no. Real Kente is made out of narrow (3" to 4" wide) woven strips, with intricate geometric designs that are stitched together along the selvage to make larger cloth. Locally grown, spun, and dyed cotton yarn used to be widely used, but today, most Kente is made with commercially produced rayon, lurex, or (much rarer) silk threads. Other fabrics with Kente-inspired designs are also called Kente, a description that makes academics and "purists" cringe. These fabrics, mostly printed cottons and rayons, are not covered in this chapter. All of the information I present in this chapter relates to the strip woven cloth from Ghana and Togo.

Roller-printed Kente at the Kumase market.

Strips of woven Kente.

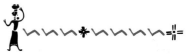

Kente cloth is made by the Ashanti people of Ghana and the Ewe of Ghana and Togo. The Ashanti live in central-southern Ghana, and their capital is Kumasi. Ashanti society is matrilineal, giving the Queen Mother great power and prestige in selecting the king, known as the Ashantihene.

The Ewe are scattered throughout eastern Ghana and southwestern Togo. There are three principal Ewe groups, each with distinct weaving traditions. The Anlo Ewe, who live in south and eastern coastal regions of Ghana, are the most dominant group. The second is the Adangbe, who live north of the Anlo, in a border region straddling Ghana and Togo. The third group, which lives north of the Anlo and Adangbe near the town of Kpandu, is known as the Central Ewe.

What's in a Name?

Neither the Ashanti nor Ewe use the word "kente" to describe their woven cloth. The Ashanti use "nsaduaso," and the Anlo Ewe use "adanuvor"; however, both people use the word Kente as a generic description of their woven cloth. No one's really sure about the origins and meaning of the word Kente, but a popular meaning adopted by African Americans is "that which will not tear."

Some female weavers are self-taught, but a few get instruction from male weavers. Skilled male weavers belong to craft guilds, while female weavers can't join guilds (but some have formed cooperatives).

Making Kente Cloth

* *Apprenticed boys wind skeins of thread onto bobbins.*
* *The weaver lays the warp threads, and then threads the heddles.*
* *Using shuttles, the weaver lays the designs.*
* *Areas of special detail may be hand-picked.*

X Making Kente: Men's Work

Kente weaving is men's work, although Ashanti women have started breaking down this bastion of male domination. Boys start learning to weave at an early age, apprenticing under their fathers or a master weaver, whom the father selects.

Most weaving is done outdoors on wooden looms. Among the Ashanti, weaving is a social undertaking. Weavers sit together, chat, and laugh while working. Strict Ewe traditions dictate that weavers isolate themselves while they work; today, however, weavers can be found working together.

Weaving Kente is labor intensive. Boys (as young as 5), who are learning to weave, wind skeins of thread onto bobbins. They must wind enough thread to lay the warp, use in shuttles, and for hand stitching. The weaver places the bobbins on the warp layer and lays enough warp for the final cloth (up to 24 strips in a typical man's cloth). Each thread is laid in a set order to create the desired warp-stripe pattern.

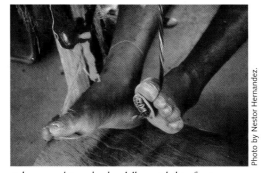

Photo by Nestor Hernandez.

A boy working the heddles with his feet.

Photo by Doran H. Ross.

A young boy winding two skeins of yarn onto a single bobbin for a double thread weft.

Next, the weaver threads the heddles. Both the Ashanti and the Ewe use at least two pairs of heddles. Each heddle is attached to its mate with a cord that passes through a pulley. At the bottom of each cord are toeholds that the weaver uses to raise and lower either pair of heddles depending on where he is in the design.

The entire warp rig consists of two pairs of heddles with pulleys, the reed, breast beam, and threaded and partially woven warp. The Ashanti and Ewe both have portable looms that can be taken indoors at the end of the day and permanent looms that can't be moved once installed.

Weavers use bobbins in shuttles to lay the weft design. To weave plain strips of cloth, the weaver passes the shuttle back and forth through the warp threads. After several back and forth passes, he pulls the reed toward himself to evenly pack the weft threads.

The Ashanti and Ewe use different techniques for their complex design areas. In Ashanti Kente, after weaving a fixed length of plain cloth, determined with a *sududua* (measuring stick), the weaver manipulates the heddle and starts weaving the design area called *Babadua* (the multicolored bands of weft-faced plain weave) using shuttles. After weaving a set length of *Babadua*, the weaver creates a hand-picked section called *adwen*. Following a measured length of *adwen*, the weaver completes another section of *Babadua* then returns to the plain weave warp pattern.

Seth Cophie working at an Ashanti horizontal loom. He is the son of Ghanian Samuel Cophie, a master weaver.

Passing the shuttle through the warp threads.

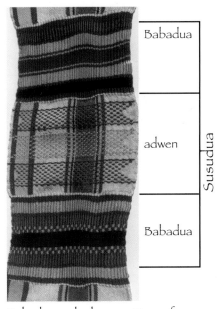

Babadua and adwen sections of Ashanti Kente.

Kente Cloth   89

Sections of Ewe Kente.

Ewe weavers also alternate sections of colored bands and hand-picked sections.

If the final cloth has a border along the long sides, the weaver must calculate where the border pattern falls on the warp as he works and make adjustments in the pattern sequence, so that the right pattern results when the strips are stitched together.

Once the weaver completes the warp, he cuts it into individual strips and stitches them together to form the cloth. Hand-stitched cloth is more prestigious among Africans, but machine-sewn cloth is common. A finished man's cloth typically measures 10 feet by 8 feet and consists of 20 to 24 10-foot long strips (this is for both Ashanti and Ewe). Depending on the complexity of a design, a weaver can take months to weave a full-length man's cloth. Ashanti women's Kente consists of three separate cloths made of 33 strips (eight in a blouse, 13 for a shawl, and 12 for a wrapped skirt), while Ewe women have up to two pieces (a blouse and a wrapper used as a skirt, or just the wrapper worn over their breasts).

Learning to Weave Kente in Africa

You can learn to weave Kente in Ghana with master weavers. Short courses (about four weeks in length) are available, and longer courses can be arranged. These courses are a great opportunity to both learn about the history and heritage of Kente weaving in Ghana and develop your skills (see Resources for more information).

Men and boys wearing Kente.

X Making Kente: A Picture Story of Ewe Kente

1
Dyed yarn drying.

2
A young boy winding the bobbin.

3
Master weaver Gilbert "Bobbo" Ahiagble threading a heddle.

4

Laying the warp thread.

5

Bobbo laying the warp thread.

Bobbo weaving.

6

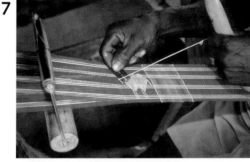
7
Hand-picking design in the weft.

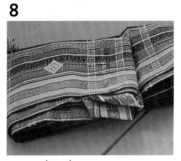
8
A completed strip.

9

Bobbo stitching strips together by machine.

All photos by Nestor Hernandez.

X Ashanti Kente: A Royal Textile

Kente is the royal court cloth. All others used it at the discretion of and with the goodwill of the king, the Ashantihene, who (according to folklore) has the clever spider Ananse to thank for teaching the Ashanti to weave!

In the mid-seventeenth century, two brothers were hunting in the forest when they came upon Ananse weaving a web. The brothers were fascinated and observed him for a while, and then decided to copy the spider's efforts. Once they had mastered the art, they returned to Bonwire village to present their new skill to their chief, who directed them to make haste and present their work to the Ashantihene Nana Osei Tutu. The king was so impressed that he made Kente the royal court cloth, forging the link between Kente and the royal court that exists to this day (although the royal grasp on weaving is now much weaker). Many of the Ashantihene's personal patterns are simply copied today, but in earlier times, no one would dare to commission a cloth with patterns held by the court without permission.

THE LOVE OF COLOR

The brightly colored, vividly patterned cloth typically considered Kente is Ashanti Kente. The bright reds, yellow, golds, and greens are desired by the Ashanti; however, earlier cloth was made from black, white, or blue cotton yarn, because these were the only dyes available. In the nineteenth century, the Ashanti started trading brightly colored silk cloth with foreign travelers. They loved the colors, but did not care for the designs, so they unraveled the silk cloth and wove the yarn into Kente. With bright colors available, weavers got more creative and made many complicated designs.

Ashanti Kente contrasts primary and secondary colors to produce cloth of extreme brilliance. They emphasize the visual tension by staggering the patterns to create checkerboard and diagonal lines throughout the cloth. Kente is used as shrouds. It is also a status garment among the Ashanti, a symbol of achievement, pride, wealth, and power typically worn or given as gifts on special occasions such as coronations, funerals, weddings, rites of passage, home comings, and thanksgivings.

Thinking about color theory and the social context of Kente, the creation of visually engaging cloth is not a fluke. Remember the saying "Clothes maketh the man?" Wealthy, status-conscious people in all societies often exhibit their social station through their attire and want to be acknowledged. So it is with the Ashanti.

I've heard people refer to the colors of Kente as "African colors." Kente colors are simply primary and secondary colors: reds, blues, golds, yellows, greens, white, and black.

The Ashanti make four qualities of Kente: plain weave, single weave, double weave, and Asasia (the most complex and prestigious Kente cloth which has a tweed-like appearance and is rarely made today).

X Colors of Ashanti Kente

The colors of Ashanti Kente also have meaning:

Black symbolizes intensified spiritual energy, communion with ancestral spirits, antiquity, spiritual maturity, and potency.

Blue denotes the blue sky, the abode of the Supreme Creator. It symbolizes spiritual sanctity, good fortune, peacefulness, harmony, and love.

Gold symbolizes royalty, wealth, elegance, high status, supreme quality, glory, and spiritual purity.

Gray symbolizes spiritual blemish and spiritual cleansing.

Green is associated with nature (vegetation, farming and harvesting, and herbal medicine). It denotes growth, vitality, fertility, prosperity, fruitfulness, abundant health, and spiritual rejuvenation.

Maroon is associated with Mother Earth, healing, and protection from evil spirits.

Pink is seen as red, rendered mild and gentle, and is associated with female essence of life. It denotes tenderness, calmness, pleasantness, and sweetness.

Purple is viewed similarly as maroon and is mostly worn by females.

Red symbolizes heightened spiritual outlook and political attitude, sacrifice, and struggle.

Silver denotes the moon and symbolizes serenity, purity, and joy.

White symbolizes spiritual purification, healing, sanctification rites, and festive occasions.

Yellow symbolizes sanctity, preciousness, royalty, wealth, spirituality, vitality, and fertility.

Source: Kwaku Ofori-Ana, Associate Professor of African History, Dept. of Fine Arts, Howard University, Washington, D.C.

X Talking Cloth: What Ashanti Kente Says

As with many African fabrics, each Kente has a name. The Ashanti name the finished cloth for the warp design (the exception is Asasia cloths, which is named for its weft patterns), but the weft designs also have names. There are over 300 Kente patterns, with weavers creating new ones every day. day. Most weavers today can name only the popular designs, so it is left to academics to research the names of other cloth.

The Ashanti name cloth after famous people (for instance popular kings or queens), things from nature (like trees and plants), and to express proverbs or social commentary. Cloth is created after significant events as a way of recording history; for example, the cloth "There is fire between two factions of the Oyoko clan" was created when civil war broke out after the death of the great king Osei Tutu.

Cloth names change to reflect the times; for instance, when President Kwame Nkrumah married his Egyptian wife Fathia, a cloth was designed and named *"Fathia befits Nkrumah."* When he was deposed, the name was changed to *"One man does not rule a nation."*

Here are some popular designs and their current names. The next time you see Kente cloth, see if you can identify any of these designs.

Broken pot.

Cannon.

Cross.

Ritual container.

Sandals.

Smooth weave or draughts.

Stone house.

Stone house, fort.

X Ewe Kente: A Social Cloth

Ewe folklore also thanks a spider for teaching them weaving. Exhausted after a futile day of hunting, the Ewe hunter Togbi Se sat under a tree to rest and observed a spider weaving a web. He was fascinated and figured humans could weave too, so he went home and tried to imitate the spider by inventing a small loom, known today as the children's loom.

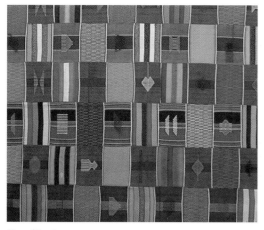

Ewe Kente.

Photo by www.africancrafts.com

Ewe Kente is different from Ashanti Kente in numerous ways. The Ewe tend not to use high-contrast, high-intensity colors, preferring instead muted browns, greens, blues, oranges, reds, and purples. The Ewe do not emphasize stark contrast between weft and warp designs; as a result, Ewe Kente is subtler, more inventive, and more rhythmic than Ashanti Kente. Ewe Kente is a quiet, well-integrated cloth. The Ewe sometimes weave familiar images of objects and animals such as combs, pineapples, stools, and parrots into their cloth.

The Ewe are less concerned with status than the Ashanti, but wear Kente for special occasions similar to their celebrations. They commemorate life stations with special cloth, such as the birth of twins, widowhood, puberty, engagement for marriage, and motherhood.

X Names of Ewe Kente

The Ewe also name their cloth. Names can be complex, philosophical, historical, related to design elements, or purely whimsical as in these examples of cloth names: The Shell of the Tortoise, Heaven and Earth, A Big Stool does not make One an important King, and You are the Winner. There is nothing hard and fast about cloth names; they change all of the time, and it's not uncommon that weavers and cloth traders disagree on a name. Ewe Kente differs from Ashanti Kente in that it can include representational motifs in the cloth. Here are some of the motifs and their meanings:

Chameleon: The world is like a chameleon's skin, it changes (no condition is permanent).

Crocodile: The crocodile does not drown in a river (I am invincible).

Elephant: I am as big as the elephant (I am invincible).

Tortoise and Snail: We do not point guns at each other (we live in peace).

Lion: I am the king.

Key: When I lock it, no one can open it (I am the ultimate authority).

Hat: He who removes his hat can travel the world with ease (the meek shall inherit the earth).

Bird: A bird that grows feathers will always fly (a child that survives infancy will always be somebody).

Rooster: The rooster says to be afraid is to live (live cautiously).

Dagger: I have two sharp edges (I am invincible).

Pineapple: You cannot get to the pineapple without being pricked by its thorns (no pain, no gain).

Leaf: I will not survive if I am plucked from a tree (I am one who depends on others).

Source: Ross, Doran H. *Wrapped in Pride: Ghanaian Kente and African American Identity.* UCLA Fowler Museum of Cultural History, 1998.

X Where to Buy Kente Cloth

In North America and Europe, Ashanti Kente is more common than Ewe Kente. Look for Kente at specialty (independent) fabric stores, bead stores, specialty galleries, and stores that carry African and ethnic artifacts (like museum shops). Cultural festivals are also a good source for Kente cloth. Mail-order sources for African fabrics may also carry Kente cloth. On the Internet, do a keyword search for Kente cloth to find vendors, or bid on auction sites like ebay. Buying Kente cloth from mail-order or Internet sources has one drawback: you may not be able to select your cloth yourself; the vendor selects what he or she thinks you would like! Because each cloth is unique, you may have preferred another piece, so check the vendor's return policies.

In the United States, Kente cloth is most commonly sold in strips, but you can buy it in larger pieces that range from "shawl-size" to large "men's cloths." Some vendors may agree to sell single strips from larger pieces, so ask.

For both Ashanti and Ewe Kente, prices will vary by the cloth's design and quality and the vendor's discretion. Strips can start at about $15, with shawls being at least $45. Expect to pay hundreds, or even thousands, of dollars for a full size "man's cloth," which averages 2-1/2 yards x 4 yards. Nothing is firm about these prices; it really depends on the artisan and vendor. Some vendors might even be willing to bargain, particularly at summer street fairs, so don't hesitate to ask.

Where to Buy Kente Cloth

- Specialty (independent) fabric stores
- Bead stores
- Specialty galleries
- Museum shops
- Cultural festivals
- Mail-order sources
- Internet

Buying Kente in Africa

If you want to purchase Kente in Africa, and you are in Accra, Ghana's capital, go to the Textile Market, or catch a tour bus to Bonwire, the official center of Ashanti Kente production. Weavers offer their stunning creations at their stores and in the markets. Commission your own cloth if you have time! You can buy Ewe Kente at the Agbozume market, which is on the highway

Kente on sale at the Textile Market in Accra.

Photo by Doran H. Ross.

from Accra (near the Togo border). It is one of the most important centers for hand-woven cloth in West Africa. You must go early: market gates open as early as 5:00 a.m., and by 9:00 a.m. most activity is over. Be aware that you will be buying Ewe "market cloth," which is— in Ewe opinion—inferior to "home cloth." Home cloth, which is more prestigious and expensive, is usually commissioned from special weavers.

X Buying Kente Cloth: What to Look for

There are several aspects of quality, aesthetic and technical, to look for when purchasing Ashanti and Ewe Kente cloth.
• Buy cloth that appeals to you (consider the yarn, weight, and aesthetics).
• Look for colors that make you look good.
• Be aware of worn or torn cloth and holes.
• Check if the strips are secure.

AESTHETICS

Do you like the patterns and colors of the cloth? If you're buying cloth that has bright primary and secondary colors, make sure they work for you. If the colors complement your skin tones, you will look great, but if they don't, the results could be disastrous. If you don't know which colors work for you, you should have a color analysis done (see page 67).

You should also consider the message in the cloth. Remember that many patterns have meanings, so ask the vendor if he or she knows. If you live outside of Ghana and Togo, it's unlikely that you'll meet many people who can "read" your cloth, but if you can, you can share this information with friends and family.

YARN INFLUENCES QUALITY AND PRICE

Silk Kente is the most desirable, but it is expensive and rare, and hand-spun and dyed cotton can also be costly. Commercially produced yarn, such as rayon, produces a cloth with a smoother, shinier look than hand-spun cotton, but the uneven, rugged look of hand-spun cotton can be quite appealing. (You can use the same methods for either type of yarn; see page 101 for more information on care.)

WEIGHT ALSO INFLUENCES PRICE

To the Ashanti, heavier cloth (with more complex woven designs) is more desirable and expensive, so expect to pay more for these pieces.

INSPECT THE CLOTH FOR FRAYED THREADS, TEARS, AND HOLES

When shopping for Kente cloth, keep in mind that older pieces may have worn areas and holes, while newer pieces shouldn't have too many. If you decide to purchase a cloth with holes, bargain for a lower price. If you buy cloth with frayed sections or holes, position your pattern to avoid these areas.

Frayed sections on Kente cloth.

SECURED STRIPS

If you are buying large pieces, check whether the strips are securely attached. Note the quality of stitching; if threads have broken, you'll have to repair or avoid these areas in your design. Hand-stitched cloth is most desired in Africa, but does not appear to have the same caché elsewhere. If the vendor claims the cloth is an antique, consult an expert before you buy (see Resources).

Be aware that the selvage edge of Kente strips may have slight indentations at the weft design areas. These don't detract from the quality; simply accommodate this in your sewing.

Before You Cut

* Preshrink your fabric.
* Avoid holes or frayed areas.
* Secure strips.

X Sewing Kente Cloth

Kente stitches easily. Set your machine to suit the weight of the fabric; most often, this will be for a medium-weight fabric.

Cut edges, particularly in the weft design sections, may unravel with normal handling during sewing if the cut edges are not secured. Finish cut edges with zigzag or serging before assembly. You may also fuse Kente with light interfacing before cutting, which will keep the threads together during sewing.

PRESHRINKING

Wash or dry clean your Kente cloth before you cut and sew to remove shrinkage. For guidance on washing or dry cleaning cloth, see the next page.

FINISHING SEAMS

Trim away any excess fabric. You can serge, zigzag, or pink raw edges, but Fray Chek also works. Joined seams can be pressed open.

Serged edge.

Zigzag stitching.

Fray Chek on the raw edge.

Pinked raw edge.

✗ Sewing Kente Cloth to Other Fabrics

You can sew Kente cloth to lots of other fabrics, including silk, linen, cotton, and suede. You shouldn't experience any problems when combining these fabrics.

SEWING NOTIONS AND OTHER THINGS

Here are some useful notions and other considerations for sewing Kente cloth.
- Needle. Use a universal size 65/9, 70/10, or 80/12, depending on the fabric's thickness.
- Thread. Use cotton-covered polyester or silk thread.
- Underlining. You can use organza, china silk, or rayon, depending on the desired hand.
- Interfacing. If you so desire, sew-in or fusible interfacing can be used, depending on the desired hand.

Kente interfaced with Armo weft.

✗ Caring for Kente Cloth

You can wash Kente cloth, by either hand or machine. Hand wash Kente cloth in cold water with a mild detergent (i.e. Ivory or Woolite), or machine wash it using a gentle cycle if the yarn is suitable. To determine the type of yarn your fabric is made of, do a flame test. (For information on performing such a test, see *Sewing Secrets from the Fashion Industry*, edited by Susan Huxley, Rodale Press, 1996.)

Kente Cloth Can Be

- *Dry cleaned*
- *Hand washed*
- *Machine washed*

Do not place in the dryer. Lay flat or line dry.

If you dry clean, select a dry cleaner that is experienced with specialty textiles and can handle Kente cloth. I have washed and dry cleaned Kente without problems; however, if you have a special piece of cloth or are wary, consult an expert for advice (see Resources).

Hand-dyed Kente could bleed, so wash it separately (most cloth is hand-dyed).

To dry Kente cloth, lay it flat or hang it, but do not place in the dryer (depending on the yarn, the fabric may shrivel).

STORING KENTE CLOTH

There are no special considerations for storing Kente cloth. Simply fold and add it to your fabric pile.

PRESSING

Kente cloth presses easily. Set your iron to the appropriate temperature for the yarn. If you are not sure of the yarn type, cut off a corner and do the flame yarn test (see page 101).

X Design Ideas

Much controversy reigns between purists and "cultural promoters" over popular uses of Kente cloth. Purists say Kente's royal heritage should limit its use to grand occasions and special garments, whereas cultural promoters say Kente can be used for anything that evokes African or African American culture and pride. With Kente patterns emblazoned on everything from bags to umbrellas, cultural promoters have probably won this battle. Its popularity peaked in the United States in the mid-1990s, when it was commonly used as stoles. While that use evoked cultural pride, it never explored other uses for the cloth.

You can use Kente cloth in men's, women's, and children's clothing (vests are most common), home furnishings, and accessories. Adult garments such as dresses, coats, skirts, and jackets require several yards of cloth, which can be quite expensive; however, you can use smaller quantities such as shawls and strips to create stunning designs. The fashions I show here require shawls and strips of Kente cloth simply to illustrate that a little goes a long way. But don't limit yourself to these ideas; if you have larger pieces of Kente, you can certainly design garments around them.

SELECTING PATTERNS

Price may limit most of us to using only strips of Kente in our designs. Don't worry; you can still make great fashions using Kente strips as a trim on collars, cuffs, hems, shawls, pillows, and table runners. With shawls or large "men's cloths," you can make entire garments, including tank tops, skirts, and jackets. The cloth will vary from medium- to heavy-weight depending on the yarn. These weights are suitable for softly structured to structured garments. Remember that you will have to match repeats at the seamlines and features such as pockets and jacket fronts, which requires extra fabric for any design you may select. Apply your knowledge about matching plaids and checks when working with repeats in Kente.

LINING

Rayon, silk, and synthetic linings are suitable depending on your personal preference. I advise lining your Kente cloth garments because lined garments last longer and wear better than those that are unlined.

COMBINING KENTE WITH OTHER FABRICS

Kente combines well with many fabrics, including raw silk, hemp, dupioni silk, cotton, taffeta, and silk charmeuse. By combining it with other fabrics, you can create interesting textural and visual contrasts. Kente's color palette gives you another opportunity to create visual contrasts. With a bit of imagination, you can use this palette to your advantage and create unique fashions. Consider the care method when you utilize Kente with other fabrics. Will you dry clean? Wash? Line dry? (For example, if you combine Kente with dupioni silk, it's best to dry clean the finished piece.)

Wear your favorite Kente as a shawl.

Model: Lisa Scott. Photo by Kim Johnson.

Silk charmeuse and Kente shawl.

Design by Ronke Luke-Boone. Photo by Kim Johnson.

SHAWLS

A shawl is a striking way to wear Kente, especially unusual pieces of cloth or antique pieces. Secure your shawl with a favorite pin.

Trim a silk charmeuse shawl with Kente strips for a touch of detail. You'll look beautiful at any special occasion! (See page 116 for instructions on making this shawl.)

Raw silk, dupioni silk, and Kente cloth blend perfectly together. I made the matching dupioni silk handbag to complete the outfit. Design by Claude Montana (Vogue 1698).

Model: Lisa Scott. Photos by John Rusnak.

DRESSES AND SUITS

In clothing, obvious places to use Kente cloth strips are pockets, hems, cuffs, and collars on dresses and jackets. These are simple ways to incorporate Kente into your wardrobe that require little cloth.

You can make fashionable outfits such as this silk suit that I trimmed around the sleeve and jacket hems with Kente cloth. Even though there is a lot of vibrant color and different patterns in this outfit, they are visually pleasing rather than jarring. The secret to this garment's success is the color combination. Yellow and red are primary colors that work well together. Green is red's complementary color on the color wheel, so those two colors work together. The Kente cloth is also red, green, and yellow. For the suit, I used a raw silk in an acid green that has yellow undertones, so it blends well with the yellow in the Kente cloth. The pattern in the Kente is fairly muted and blends with the plaid in the dupioni silk blouse. This suit is a great example of skillful use of color and pattern.

Design Insight

◈ *Understand and use the color wheel to your advantage.*
◈ *Create visual contrast by combining patterns.*
◈ *Small amounts of Kente can have a big impact.*

This outfit is another example of how a little Kente cloth can make a stylish outfit. I also exploited color and textile contrasts in this design. The secret to the success is the harmony between the green, red, and yellow. This style—a blouse over a long skirt—is similar to popular two-piece outfits African women wear, but here I update the idea using silk, modern Kente designs, brighter colors, and clean style lines. The blouse is made out of dupioni silk and trimmed with Kente, called Unity and made by Bobbo, an Ewe master weaver. I incorporated the fringe ends of the Kente strip into my design. The skirt is a washable sueded silk.

Design by Ronke Luke-Boone. Model: Karina El-Halabi. Photos by Kim Johnson.

Simple lines and a great color contrast are the perfect backdrop for the Kente trim.

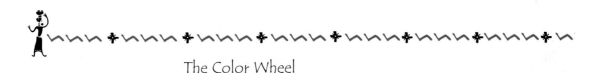

The Color Wheel

Understanding color is a great help for working skillfully with Kente cloth. The primary colors are red, yellow, and blue. You can't make primary colors, but you can use them to make an endless array of other colors starting with the secondary colors, green, orange, and purple. Yellow + Red = Orange. Blue + Red = Purple. Blue + Yellow = Green. These color recipes are a great key to knowing which colors work together. Because red and yellow are in orange, you can, generally, combine red and orange, yellow and orange, or all three colors in one project. The same applies to the other color recipes.

Complementary colors are also important to know. Green is red's complementary color, and the two work well together. Blue and orange are complementary colors, and yellow and purple are complementary to each other.

White and black aren't considered "colors" in color theory, but you can use them to mix "shades" (a color mixed with black) and "tints" (a color mixed with white). Get a color wheel from an art supply store and start playing with color. For more on color theory, consider What Every Artist Needs to Know About Paints & Colors, *by David Pyle, Krause Publications, 2000.*

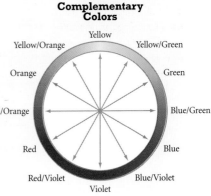

Complementary Colors

Yellow

Yellow/Orange   Yellow/Green

Orange   Green

Red/Orange   Blue/Green

Red   Blue

Red/Violet   Blue/Violet

Violet

Go beyond using Kente cloth as a trim: incorporate it as sections into your design, such as in this silk dress, where I used Kente cloth in the midriff. The color palette is complementary. The Kente cloth's patterns provide a good visual break from the red of the dupioni silk, and the colors also tie in with the plaid of the dupioni silk under dress.

Model: Lisa Scott.
Photos by Kim Johnson.

Kente cloth incorporated into the design forms a nice visual bridge between the red and plaid.

This dramatic coat shows a wonderful way to utilize an entire Kente shawl in an outfit without cutting the cloth. The Kente cloth forms a shawl collar, which can be pulled up as a hood. The Kente cloth is a vibrant contrast to the gray wool coat. The coat has shoulder ties, which allow the collar to be pulled up around the shoulders and face.

Design by Dominick Cardella, Artifactory. Model: Lisa Scott.
Photos by Kim Johnson.

Turn your shawl into a dramatic collar on a coat.

Design Insight

❖ *Select designs that allow you to use the entire piece without cutting the cloth.*

PURSES

This pretty purse is made out of a Kente strip and ribbon. It is an attractive accent to a smart outfit.

CHILDREN'S CLOTHING

Kente cloth's colors are great for children's wear, including vests, coats, trims on shirts, and dresses. More expensive Kente can be used for special occasion wear for birthdays or holidays. Combining Kente with other fabrics in children's wear is also a great idea as in these pretty girls' dresses and boys' vests.

Kente cloth and woven ribbon purse.

Design by Ronke Luke-Boone.

Kids' vests in Kente cloth.

Illustration by Karina El-Halabi.

Use Kente cloth in pretty dresses.

Illustration by Sharon Autrey.

Use Kente cloth in pretty dresses.

Illustration by Sharon Autrey.

MEN'S CLOTHING

The most popular outfits made from Kente for men are stoles, hats, caps, and vests, but you can certainly make cummerbunds, bowties, and ties.

Men cut a smart image in Kente cloth vests.

Illustrations by Karina El-Halabi.

Jazz up formal wear with a Kente bowtie and cummerbund.

Illustration by Karina El-Halabi.

HOME IDEAS

Carry an African theme through to your dining room. The Biedermeier chair at right is upholstered with Ewe Kente.

Ewe Kente placemats add charm to any table. The examples shown below right are laminated.

Pillows are a simple, easy way to add Kente cloth to your home décor. But don't simply make an entire pillow out of Kente cloth—be inventive! The very contemporary pillows out of Kente cloth and dupioni silk shown at bottom right are an example of how you can be creative. The vibrant colors of the dupioni silk and Kente cloth play off each other. These pillows would look wonderful in many décor styles including modern and ethnic themes (see page 130 for instructions on how to make Kente cloth pillows).

Louise Meyer, a Washington D.C.-based designer, custom makes very stylish vertical blinds, like those shown below, covered in Kente cloth or woven cotton strips. These are an excellent example of high-end design using traditional African textiles.

If you don't want to cut up particularly beautiful large Kente cloth, consider using it for a throw. You can wrap yourself up with a beautiful Kente and relax with a great book on a fall or winter day. Or, use a shawl as a table runner.

Design by Louise Meyer.
Photo by Nestor Hernandez.

A Biedermeier chair upholstered in Ewe Kente.

Design by Louise Meyer.

Laminated Kente cloth placemats.

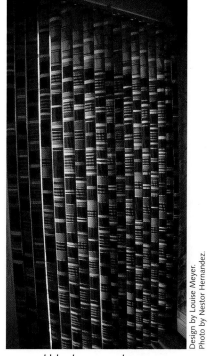

Design by Louise Meyer.
Photo by Nestor Hernandez.

Vertical blinds covered in Ewe Kente.

Design by Ronke Luke-Boone.
Photo by Kim Johnson.

Kente cloth and silk pillows.

CHAPTER 6

Projects

Now is the fun part! In this chapter, I have included fourteen different projects, ranging in difficulty from easy to more challenging. Whether you are interested in making something for yourself, your home, or a gift for a friend or family member, you are sure to find something here. Before you begin any of the projects, please read all of the instructions!

Illustration key:

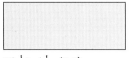

Right side (RS)

Wrong side (WS)

Project 1   Tunic With Back Kuba Panel
Difficulty Level: Intermediate

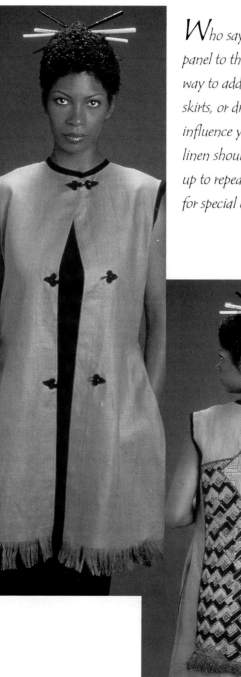

*W*ho says garment backs should be plain? Adding a beautiful Kuba panel to the back of a tunic (or jacket) is a great—and inexpensive— way to add drama to a versatile garment. Wear your tunic over pants, skirts, or dresses. Remember, the fabric you choose for your tunic will influence your care method (washing or dry cleaning). (For instance, linen should be dry cleaned, but it's not clear how Kuba cloth will hold up to repeated dry cleaning, so you may only want to wear this tunic for special occasions.)

Model: Lisa Scott.
Photos by Kim Johnson.

You Will Need

Kuba velvet panel, no larger than 16" x 24" (you may combine several into a collage*)

Muslin or sew-in stabilizer for underlining (sufficient for the size of your Kuba cloth)

3 yd. linen (45" wide) or other fabric of your choice

1 yd. interfacing for the front opening

Matching thread

3 buttons or frog closures (optional)

Purchased double-fold wide bias tape

*Collaging is a way to arrange several pieces of fabric into a single larger piece in a pleasing manner, as shown in the sample.

PATTERN PIECES ON PATTERN SHEET

Tunic Front (1)
Tunic Back (2)

Pattern pieces are provided for the following sizes.

Size	Bust (inches)
S (8-10)	33
M (12-14)	34-36
L (16-18)	37-39
XL (20-22)	45-48
XXL (24-26)	41-43

5/8" seam allowance included on pattern. Cutting lines are shown for each size.
Tunic finished length: 33"

Note: The tunic pattern covers the shoulders slightly.

CUTTING (LINEN)

Cut 2 of Tunic Front (1) on straight grain.
Cut 2 of Tunic Back (2) on fold.

1. Interface the facings on the tunic front.

2. Transfer the pattern markings to fabric.

ASSEMBLING THE TUNIC

Kuba Panel

3. Trim away the Kuba cloth's stitched hem. If the cloth has a fringed edge (as in the one shown), consider keeping it.

4. (Optional) Straighten the edges of the cloth to form a rectangle or square. Skip this step if the crooked edges appeal to you (they can add charm to your garment).

5. Cut the underlining to fit the Kuba cloth. With wrong sides together, pin and hand-baste the Kuba to the underlining.

6. Finish the Kuba panel's raw edges with a serger, or zigzag the raw edges and cover the zigzag with an embroidery stitch.

Attaching the Kuba Panel to a Back Section

7. Set one of the back pieces aside to use later as a lining. Working on a flat surface, position the Kuba cloth on the tunic back piece in a manner you like. Pin and hand baste the Kuba panel in place.

8. Machine stitch the Kuba panel to the tunic back.

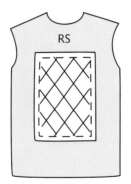

9. Working on a flat surface, with wrong sides facing, position the second back piece (the lining) over the piece you have just worked, covering the stitching. Pin and hand baste the lining in place. You will work the two pieces as one.

10. Stitch across the bottom of the back, 2" from the edge.

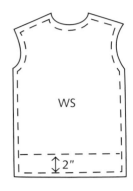

Front Facings

11. Stitch across the bottom of the tunic fronts, 2" from the hem edge.

12. Fold the facings to the inside, along the fold line. Fold again to the inside, along the facing line, encasing the raw edges. Press. Baste and stitch the facing in place, up to the stitching line, up to 2" from the hemline.

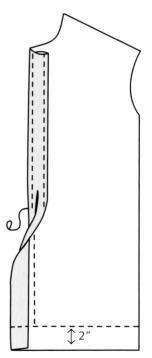

Shoulder the Seams

13. With right sides together, join the front and back pieces together at the shoulder seams. Trim and finish the seams' raw edges. Press the seams open.

Finishing the Neckline

14. Trim away a 1/2" seam around the neckline. Encase the neck edge with purchased, pre-folded bias tape as shown. Fold under the ends at the neck edges and stitch the bias tape in place.

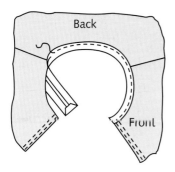

Finishing the Armholes

15. Trim away a 1/2" seam around the armholes. Encase the armholes with purchased, pre-folded bias tape as shown. Stitch the bias tape in place.

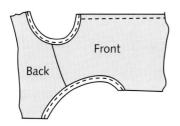

Side Seams

16. With right sides together, stitch the side seams, leaving the sides open from the waistline to the hem. Finish the side seams' raw edges, up to stitching line at the hem. Press the seams open. Topstitch the seam allowance around the open side seams.

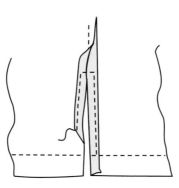

Buttons

17. Attach the buttons to the left side and make buttonholes on the right side of the tunic (see pattern for spacing). Optional: Use frog closures, as shown on the sample.

Fringe Hem

18. Pull out the crosswise threads at the hem on the tunic front and back to the stitching line to form a 2" fringe at the hem.

Project 2

Pieced Fancy Prints and Linen Jacket

Difficulty Level: Intermediate to Advanced

*Y*ou don't need a lot of fabric to make this adorable jacket out of fancy prints and linen. In fact, I made this pieced jacket out of remnants, so don't throw away your stash of leftovers! This jacket is Folkwear Pattern's Chinese Jacket (114) (see Resources). This is a great example of thinking across cultures and adapting a great pattern to fit your design ideas.

Note: You may use the principles shown here with another pattern of your choice to create a pieced jacket.

Model: Karina El-Halabi. Photo by Kim Johnson.

You Will Need

Folkwear Pattern 114, Chinese Jacket

1/4 yd. fancy or wax prints (45" wide)

1/4 yd. linen 1 (45" wide)

1 yd. linen 2 (45" wide)

Tracing paper

Matching thread

Pencil

Ruler

Purchased double-fold wide bias tape (optional)

MAKING THE FRONT JACKET PATTERN PIECES

1. Working with ruler and pencil, mark up the jacket front pattern (for View A) to the dimensions as shown.

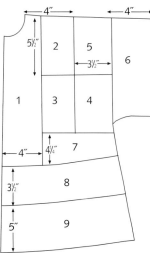

2. Place tracing paper over the pattern and trace each pattern section. Leave sufficient space around each section to add a 1/2" seam allowance.

3. Add a 1/2" seam allowance to each piece.

CUTTING OUT THE PIECES

4. Cut the jacket front from the three fabrics.

Fancy prints	Cut 2 of 3, 5, 8
Linen 1	Cut 2 of 2, 6, 7
Linen 2	Cut 2 of 1, 4, 9

5. Cut the jacket back (from View A of the pattern) out of Linen 2.

ASSEMBLING THE FRONT JACKET PIECES

6. Join the front jacket pieces together in the order shown (Steps 1-8). Finish the raw seams after each step.

7. With right sides together, stitch the jacket front and back together at the shoulder and side seams. Finish the seam edges.

FINISHING THE FRONT, NECK, BACK, AND SLEEVE EDGES

8. Using a serger, finish the front, neck, back, and sleeve edges.

9. (Optional) Encase the raw edges with purchased bias tape.

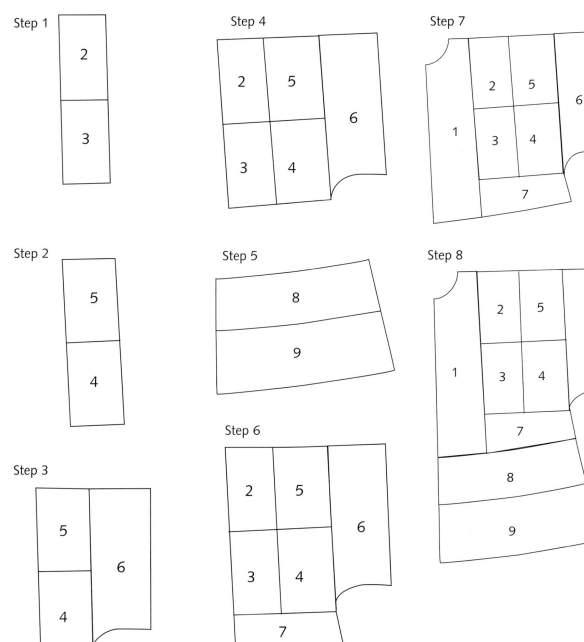

Project 3   Silk Charmeuse and Kente Shawl
Difficulty Level: Easy

Add colorful Kente strips to update a classic silk charmeuse shawl. This is a simple, yet effective, way to use small pieces of Kente. Choose a charmeuse in one color from your Kente strip. The vibrant colors of the two complement each other very well. Drape this pretty shawl over your shoulders to dress up any outfit for day or evening wear.

Design by Ronke Luke-Boone.
Photo by Kim Johnson.

You Will Need

1 yd. silk charmeuse (45" wide)

23" strip of Kente cloth

Matching thread

Note: 1/2" seam allowance included.

1. Cut the silk into four pieces along the length, into 11-1/4" x 36" strips.

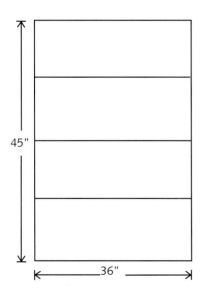

2. On two pieces, baste a placement line 3/4" from the raw edge, across the narrow width of the strips.

3. Baste and stitch Kente strips along the basted placement lines.

4. With right sides together, stitch the strips together along the short edge, opposite the Kente strips, to form a long, continuous piece. Trim the seam and press open.

Repeat with the other two strips.

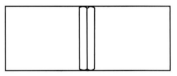

5. With right sides together, matching seamlines, stitch the long pieces made in Step 4 together, leaving an 8" opening along one edge.

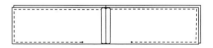

6. Trim the seam allowance. Turn the shawl to the right side. Press. Stitch the opening closed by hand or machine.

Project 4   Mudcloth Vest

Difficulty Level: Easy

Design by Ronke Luke-Boone. Model: Trina Bowen.
Photos by Kim Johnson.

A vest is a great modern way to add mud-cloth to your wardrobe when you use a more unusual mudcloth piece. In this project, we will make simple changes to a purchased pattern. Don't worry—one of the pleasures of sewing is being able to personalize patterns as you wish! Experienced sewers will have no problems with the adjustments shown here. If you are a beginner, this is great way to start to learn how to adjust patterns. For this vest, you will also practice combining several pieces of mudcloth into an attractive garment.

Note: You may use the principles shown here with another pattern of your choice.

You Will Need

City Vest Pattern (Hibiscus 1002, see Resources)

3 small pieces of mudcloth (each approx. 1 yd. in length) (Remember guidance on combining motifs, see page 19)

2 yd. linen or cotton for lining (45" wide)

2 yd. Whisper Weft fusible interfacing

Matching thread

Tracing paper

2 packets double-fold wide bias binding (contrasting or matching colors)

Iron

Serger (optional)

PREPARING THE MUDCLOTH

1. Wash the mudcloth to preshrink (see page 18). Allow to dry.

MAKING THE VEST FRONT PATTERN PIECES

Note: You will use the Vest Back sections provided in the pattern.

2. On the pattern front piece, draw a line across the width of

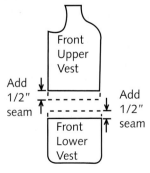

the pattern at the upper casing line. Place tracing paper over the pattern front and trace the Front Upper Vest and Front Lower Vest as shown. Leave sufficient space around the pieces to add a seam allowance. Add a 1/2" seam allowance to each section as shown.

CUTTING THE PATTERN PIECES

3. Out of lining
Cut 1 of Vest Back on Fold, as shown in pattern instructions
Cut 1 of Vest Front on Straight Grain, as shown in pattern instructions

4. Out of Mudcloth 1
Cut 2 of Front Upper Vest.

5. Out of Mudcloth 2
Cut 2 of Front Lower Vest.

Important: If you cut your mudcloth on a single layer to match motifs, you must flip the pattern over to the wrong side and lay it on the fabric before you cut. This way, you will get the left side of the vest. If you don't, you will have two right sides!

6. Out of Mudcloth 3
Cut 1 of Back on fold

7. Out of Interfacing
Cut 1 of Vest Back on fold
Cut 2 of Front Upper Vest (created in Step 2)
Cut 2 of Front Lower Vest (created in Step 2)

INTERFACING

8. Following the manufacturer's instructions, fuse interfacing to the Front Upper Vest, Front Lower Vest, and Vest Back.

ASSEMBLING THE VEST FRONT

9. With wrong sides together, raw edges even, stitch the Front Upper Vest and Front Lower Vest together. The seam will show on the right side. Finish the raw edge by serging or encasing the raw edge in bias binding. Press the seam toward the Front Lower Vest.

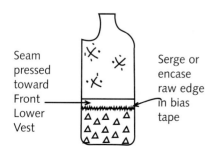

Seam pressed toward Front Lower Vest

Serge or encase raw edge in bias tape

Note: In this design, I do not press the seam open to reduce bulk as I advise in the chapter on mudcloth because I use the ridge formed by the bulk as a design element in the vest. You see, you can break the rules, as long as you make them work for you!

JOINING FRONT AND BACK OUTER

10. With the mudcloth right sides together, raw edges even, stitch together the Front and Back sections at the shoulder and side seams. Trim and press the seams open. The seam allowances are provided in the pattern instructions.

WS

JOINING FRONT AND BACK LINING

11. With the lining right sides together, raw edges even, stitch together the Front and Back sections at the shoulder and side seams. Trim and press the seams open. The seam allowances are provided in the pattern instructions.

JOINING FRONT AND BACK OUTER TO LINING

12. Position the vest outer over the vest lining, wrong sides together, matching the shoulder and side seams, and all raw edges. Baste the vest outer and lining together around the armholes and the

front, back, and bottom of the vest. Stitch the pieces together. **Note:** Baste and stitch through all fabric layers, 1/4" from the edge.

Baste

ENCASING ARM HOLE EDGES IN THE BIAS

13. Starting at the underarm, encase the raw edge within the bias. Pin in place, overlapping the start of the bias 1" at the end. Fold under the bias 1/2" at the end to cover the ends of the bias. Stitch through all thicknesses, close to the edge of the bias. Repeat for the other armhole.

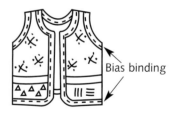

Bias binding

ENCASING THE FRONT, BACK, AND HEM EDGES IN THE BIAS

14. Starting at a side seam, encase the raw edges in the bias. Pin in place, overlapping the start of the bias 1" at the end. Fold under the bias 1/2" at the end to cover the ends of the bias. Stitch through all thicknesses, close to the bias' edge.

Project 5   Magazine Tote

Difficulty Level: Intermediate

This tote bag looks wonderful when made from mudcloth or any other fashion fabric (I used jute for this sample). If you use 1 yard of 54" fabric, you'll have enough to make both the bag and the lining.

Design by Ronke Luke-Boone.

You Will Need

1 yd. 54" fashion fabric (heavy-weight ethnic print, linen, canvas, hemp, jute, burlap, suede, or leather)

16" strip of 5" wide mudcloth

1/2 yd. craft interfacing

1-1/2 yd. piping that contrasts with fashion fabric (optional)

2-1/2 yd. 2" wide strap

9" heavy-duty zipper

16" heavy-duty zipper

29" x 14" piece foam* (optional)

3" x 12" piece firm cardboard

Matching thread

Zipper pulls (optional)

*This will give the bag a soft feel and support its sides so they are always upright.

PATTERN PIECES ON PATTERN SHEET

Magazine Tote Front & Back (1)
Magazine Tote Lower Front Pocket (2)
Magazine Tote Front Pocket Lining (3)
Magazine Tote Bag Bottom (4)
Magazine Tote Cardboard Bottom Support (5)

CUTTING PATTERN PIECES

1. Out of fashion fabric, cut:
4 Magazine Tote Front & Back
4 Magazine Tote Bag Bottom
1 Magazine Tote Lower Front Pocket
1 Magazine Tote Front Pocket Lining

2. Out of mudcloth, cut:
1 Magazine Tote Lower Front Pocket

3. Out of craft interfacing, cut:
2 Magazine Tote Front & Back
2 Magazine Tote Bag Bottom
1 Magazine Tote Lower Front Pocket

4. (Optional) Out of foam, cut:
2 pieces, each 14-1/2" x 14"

5. Out of cardboard, cut:
2 or more pieces to get a firm base

Assembling the Magazine Tote

Note: All seam allowances are 1/4".

Interfacing and Markings

6. Fuse the interfacing to the wrong sides of the pattern pieces and transfer the markings to the pattern pieces.

Front Zipper Pocket

7. Designate one of the two front and back pieces you fused with interfacing as the front. (**Note:** The remaining two pieces will be used as the lining.)

8. With right sides together, pin the front pocket lining to the bag front section, matching the dots. Baste the pocket to the bag along the zipper placement line. This is also the centerline. Stitch along a stitching line, 1/4" from the centerline, forming a rectangle around the centerline. Slash along the centerline, stopping 1/2" from the edge. Clip diagonally to rectangle the corners. Do not clip through the threads.

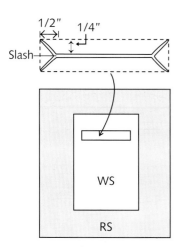

9. Turn the pocket to the inside and press (this is the zipper opening).

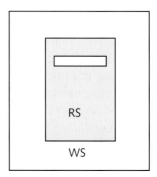

10. Shorten the 9" zipper to fit in the opening. Center the shortened zipper under the opening. Baste the zipper in place. Stitch.

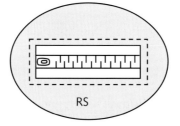

11. Turn to the inside of the bag. Fold the pocket in half, right sides together. Stitch around three edges to form the pocket "bag." Be careful not to catch the pocket to the front section.

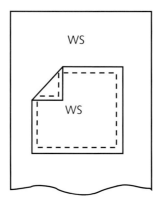

Lower Front Pocket

12. (Optional) Baste piping to the long edge of the lower front pocket.

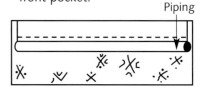

13. With right sides together, stitch the mudcloth pocket outer to the lining along the long edge (over optional piping). Open pocket out. Press the seam allowance toward the lining and understitch on the lining. Fold in half and press. Baste the pocket's unfinished short edges together.

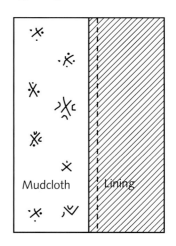

14. Matching dots, baste the lower front pocket to the bottom of the bag front section along the sides and bottom.

Reinforcing the Front and Back Sections

15. Reinforce the lower edge of the front and back

sections at the large dots. Clip to the dots.

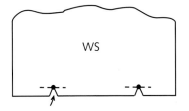

Note: On the bag front, you will reinforce through the lower pocket.

STRAPS

16. Cut the strap into two halves. Turn under 1" at each end. Attach one strap to the bag's front section and one to the back, centering the straps over the dotted line between the dots.

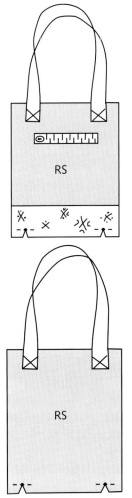

ZIPPERS

17. Shorten the 16" zipper to fit the bag's top edge within the seam allowance.

18. With right sides together, stitch one of the zipper's long edges to the front's top edge and the zipper's other long edge to the back's top edge.

SIDE SEAMS

19. With the front and back bag sections right sides together, stitch the side seams.

BOTTOM

20. (Optional) Baste piping to the right side of the bag bottom section (the interfaced section). **Note:** You will have to clip piping at the corners in order to pivot it.

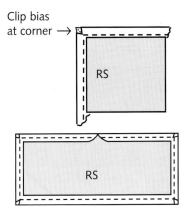

Clip bias at corner →

21. With right sides together, pin the bag bottom to the lower edge of the bag front and back, matching dots. Stitch, pivoting at the outer dots to form a rectangular bottom.

LINING: SIDE SEAMS AND BOTTOM

22. Reinforce the lower edge of the front and back lining sections at the large circles, as you did with the outer pieces. Clip to the circles. With right sides together, stitch the side seams of the front and back lining sections.

23. Pin the bottom lining to the lower edge of the bag front and back lining, matching dots. Stitch around two short and one long edge, pivoting at the dots to form a rectangular bottom. Leave the area between two dots on one of the long edges open so that you have an opening to turn the bag to right side out.

ATTACHING LINING TO BAG OUTER

24. With right sides together, insert the outer bag into the lining. Stitch together around the upper edge.

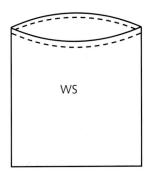

25. Turn to the right side through the lining's opening. Press. Topstitch close to the zipper.

26. (Optional) Insert foam into the bag through the lining's opening. Position the foam between the lining and outer bag. Make sure the foam lies flat.

27. Close the lining (slip-stitch or by machine). Insert the lining into the bag.

CARDBOARD BASE

28. With right sides together, raw edges even, stitch around three sides of the remaining bag bottom pieces, leaving the area between the two dots open. Turn to the right side and press.

29. Insert cardboard through the opening. Slipstitch or machine stitch the opening closed. Insert the bottom into the bag.

ZIPPER PULLS

30. Add a personal touch to your bag by adorning the zipper pulls with beads, tassels, or any decoration of your choice.

Project 6   Waist Pouch

Difficulty Level: Easy to Intermediate

You Will Need

5" x 10" strip mudcloth

1/4 yd. canvas (45" wide)

1/4 yd. cotton lining (45" wide)

1/4 yd. craft interfacing

2 yd. 1" wide cotton webbing (You may require more to ensure a comfortable fit around your waist)

12" zipper

1 side release buckle

1 strap adjuster

Matching thread

Model: Karina El-Halabi.
Photo by Kim Johnson.

Waist pouches are very popular, especially on vacations—you can carry all of your basic stuff and keep your hands free. There's no need to keep this functional accessory plain. By jazzing it up with mudcloth, you'll create a smart, fashionable accessory.

CUTTING

Waist Pouch Front and Back	Waist Pouch Upper Band	Waist Pouch Lower Band	Strap Carrier
Cut 1 of mudcloth	Cut 2 of canvas	Cut 1 of canvas	Cut 4 of canvas
Cut 1 of canvas	Cut 2 of cotton lining	Cut 1 of cotton lining	Cut 2 of interfacing
Cut 2 of cotton lining	Cut 2 of interfacing	Cut 1 of interfacing	
Cut 2 of interfacing			

Note: 1/2" seam allowance included.

PATTERNS ON PATTERN SHEET

Waist Pouch Front and Back
Waist Pouch Upper Band
Waist Pouch Strap Carrier
Waist Pouch Lower Band

TRANSFER MARKINGS

The + denotes the center point on each side.

ASSEMBLING THE WAIST POUCH

Interfacing

1. Fuse the interfacing to the mudcloth and canvas pieces.

2. With wrong sides together, baste the cotton lining to each section to cover the interfacing. (The front section is shown.)

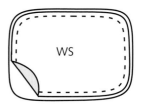

WS

Note: For the remainder of the instructions, the cotton lining is the wrong side and the canvas or mudcloth side is the right side.

Strap Carrier

3. Cut a 14" strip of 1" wide webbing. Slip the webbing through the receiving end of the buckle. Fold the webbing in half. With raw edges even, and right sides together, match the center point of the webbing and strap carrier as shown. Baste in place.

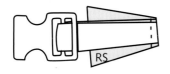

4. With raw edges even, and right sides together, match the center point of the remaining webbing and strap carrier as shown. Baste in place.

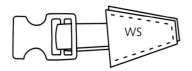

5. Slip the webbing through the strap adjuster and through the prong end of the buckle. Loop the webbing back through the buckle and the strap adjuster as shown. Try on and adjust the length as necessary. Cut off any excess webbing. Stitch the end in place (a zigzag stitch is suitable).

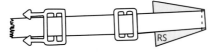

6. With right sides together, stitch the strap carrier sections together as shown.

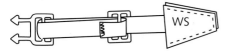

7. Attach the completed strap carriers to the waist pouch back, positioning the carriers at the center of the back piece.

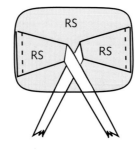

Zipper

8. On the long edge of each upper band, press under a 1/2" seam.

9. Baste the zipper to the folded edges of each upper band section. Stitch in place.

Upper and Lower Bands

10. With right sides together, matching center points, attach the upper and lower bands to form one continuous piece. Press the seams toward the lower band.

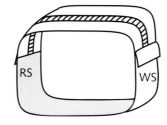

Joining the Pieces

11. With right sides together, match the center points of the band with those of the outer bag mudcloth section. **Note:** The cotton lining side is the wrong side.

12. Baste the band to the outer front section. Clip the band to ease fullness around the curves of the outer front section as necessary. Stitch the outer front and band together.

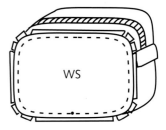

13. Open the zipper. With right sides together, matching raw edges and center points, baste the band to the waist pouch back section. Clip the bands and ease fullness around the curves. Stitch in place.

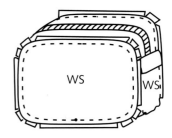

14. Turn to the right side.

Project 7   Barrettes

Difficulty Level: Easy

Hair barrettes made from Kente cloth, wax prints, or fancy prints are a pretty, colorful accent for any girl or woman. They are very simple to make and don't require a lot of fabric, so they are a great way to use up remnants. They also make great gift ideas and stocking stuffers.

Kente Cloth Version

You Will Need

8" piece Kente strip

4" piece 1/2" wide matching or contrasting ribbon

1 plain metal barrette

Matching thread

Iron

Glue gun

Serger (optional)

1. Finish the Kente strip's raw edges using a satin stitch, zigzag, or serger.

2. Fold the strip in half and press to mark the center.

3. Baste along this center crease.

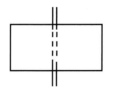

4. Pull the basting thread to gather the Kente. Wrap threads around the center and tighten to form the bow. Knot the thread ends.

5. Wrap the ribbon around the center of the bow, concealing threads. Secure the ribbon ends on the underside with the glue gun. Cut off any excess ribbon.

6. Apply a layer of glue onto the top of the barrette. Press the bow into place while the glue is still hot. Allow to dry.

Fancy or Wax Prints Version

You Will Need

1/4 yd. fancy prints or wax prints

(Optional) 4" piece 1/2" wide matching or contrasting ribbon

1 barrette

Matching thread

Iron

Glue gun

1. From the fabric, cut two 5" x 9" pieces for the bow front and back and one 1" x 4" strip for the ribbon (or use optional ribbon).

2. Fold over a 1/2" seam along the strip's long edges. Press in place.

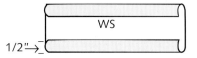

3. With right sides together, sew the bow front and back together (with a 1/2" seam allowance), leaving a 1-1/2" to 2" opening in the bottom. Trim seam allowance to 1/4".

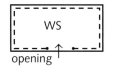

4. Turn the bow to the right side through the opening. Press. Stitch the opening closed by hand or machine.

5. Repeat Steps 2 to 6 on the previous page (Kente version) to complete your bow. If you are using the cotton

strip from Step 2, use this piece in Step 6. If using ribbon, proceed as stated.

VARIATIONS ON THE BASIC BOW

You may make many variations on the basic bow. Here are some ideas.

SHAPED BOW

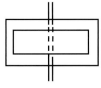

To make the shaped bow, in Step 1, cut two pieces to the dimensions shown for the front and back.

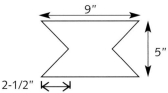

Follow Step 2. After stitching the front and back together in Step 3, clip to the point as shown. Be careful not to clip the thread. Turn to the right side.

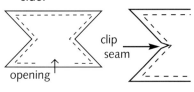

Follow the remaining instructions to complete the shaped bow.

DOUBLE BOW

To make the double bow, cut two 5" x 9" pieces for the larger bow and two 3" x 7" pieces for the smaller bow.

Follow Steps 3 and 4 for each bow. Center the small bow over the large one. Baste together and continue with Steps 5 and 6 on the previous page (Kente version).

DOUBLE-SHAPED BOW

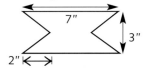

To make the double-shaped bow, cut two 5" x 9" pieces for the larger bow and two pieces for the smaller bow in the following dimensions.

Follow Steps 3 and 4 for the large bow. For the small bow, stitch the front and back together as in Step 3 and clip to the point as shown at left. Be careful not to clip the thread. Turn to the right side. Center the small bow over the large one. Baste together and continue with Steps 5 and 6 on the previous page (Kente version).

Project 8   Korhogo Floor Pillow

Difficulty Level: Easy

You Will Need

1 piece Korhogo cloth (at least 26" x 26")

1 yd. matching or contrasting linen for pillow back

2 yd. 1" grid paper (or rotary cutter and mat)

Armo weft interfacing

Matching thread

24" x 24" purchased pillow form

*P*illows are a popular use for Korhogo cloth. If you have large panels or oversized motifs on your cloth, consider making floor pillows; these are functional accents that provide additional seating in your living area. Oversized pillows also look wonderful as a daytime accent on your bed. These pillows—shown with two fancy prints pillows—are an inviting addition to this window bench.

MAKING THE PATTERN PIECES

1. Pillow front: Using 1" grid paper, cut a 25" x 25" square.

2. Pillow back: Using 1" grid paper, cut two pieces, one 12" x 25" and one 17" x 25".
Note: 1/2" seam allowance included.
Note: If you own a rotary cutter and mat, you can cut the fabric without making patterns.

CUTTING THE PIECES

3. Pillow front: Study the Korhogo cloth to find motif groupings you like. Using the pattern, cut the pillow front.

4. Pillow back: Using the two pattern pieces, cut one of each from linen.

ASSEMBLING THE PILLOW

5. Fuse the entire back of the pillow front with interfacing.

6. Turn under a long edge of one back section 1/4". Turn under another 1/4" and stitch. Repeat with the other back section.

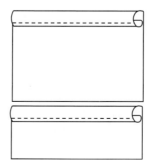

7. With right sides together, pin the front and back together, overlapping the back pieces as shown. Stitch the front and back together. Finish (serge or zigzag) the raw edges.

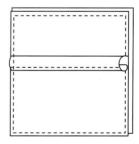

8. Turn the pillow to right side. Press. Insert the pillow form.

Project 9   Kuba Throw Pillow
Difficulty Level: Easy

Photo by Kim Johnson.

Kuba velvets (the embroideries) are most commonly used for throw pillows in the United States, Canada, and Europe. Pillows are a simple project to show off the dazzling embroidery on Kuba cloth. The cloth's neutral palette makes these throw pillows a perfect accent to many rooms with a contemporary or ethnic style. Pillows are also an easy project for beginners working with Kuba cloth. You get a feel for the cloth without tackling complicated sewing ventures. Once you're comfortable making pillows, only your imagination will limit what you can make with Kuba cloth.

A note about this project: I do not provide specific dimensions for the size of Kuba velvet you must use because they come in so many varying sizes. Find a piece you like and measure off a square or rectangle to the dimensions you wish. Note those dimensions. You will cut your pillow back and front underlining to fit these dimensions. Don't worry—you can do it!

You Will Need

1 embroidered Kuba velvet (any size)

Linen or raw silk, enough for pillow back (one and one-half times the size of the Kuba velvet)

Cotton muslin, enough to underline the Kuba velvet and make a pillow insert (if you are not using purchased insert)

1" grid paper (at least twice the size of the Kuba velvet)

Matching thread

Pillow filling or purchased pillow insert.

Note: 1/2" seam allowance included.

MAKING THE PATTERN PIECES

1. Measure the Kuba cloth to determine the approximate size of the square or rectangle. Note these measurements.

2. Using the 1" grid paper, draw a true square (or rectangle) to these dimensions. This is the pillow front pattern. Make the pattern large enough to use up the entire piece of cloth. **Note:** This pattern will include a seam allowance.

3. For the pillow back, draw two pattern sections: one pattern section three-quarters the size of the front and one pattern section one-quarter the size of the front.

CUTTING THE PILLOW PIECES

4. Examine the cloth's design to find an orientation you like. Using the front pattern, cut one pillow front out of the Kuba cloth and muslin.

5. Using the back patterns, cut the back pieces out of linen or raw silk.

ASSEMBLING THE PILLOW

6. To underline the pillow front, place the muslin on the wrong side of the Kuba cloth. Pin in place with edges even. Hand-baste in place. Serge or zigzag the cut edge to prevent unraveling during assembly.

7. Turn under a long edge of the larger back section 1/4". Turn under another 1/4" and stitch. Repeat with the other back section.

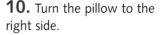

8. Finish each back section's remaining raw edges (serge or zigzag).

9. With right sides together, edges even, stitch the front and back sections together as shown (1/4" seam allowance). Finish cut edges.

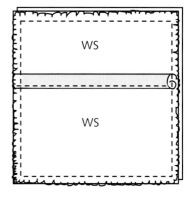

10. Turn the pillow to the right side.

PILLOW INSERT

11. If you are not using a purchased pillow insert the size of your Kuba pillow, you will have to make one. Using the pattern, cut two front sections out of muslin. Stitch together, leaving an opening in one side. Turn to the right side. Stuff the pillow with pillow filling to the desired thickness. Close the opening using a slipstitch.

12. If you are using a purchased pillow insert, put it in the Kuba pillow.

Project 10 Kente Pillow

Difficulty Level: Easy

You can make these stunning pillows with a single strip of Kente! You don't need much fabric to create modern fashions with an "ethnic" touch. These pillows are made with dupioni silk and Kente cloth. Don't be afraid to try these combinations; the vibrant colors of both fabrics bounce off of each other.

Design by Ronke Luke-Boone.
Photo by Kim Johnson.

You Will Need

1/2 yd. dupioni silk

13" piece Kente strip

1/2 yd. decorative trim

12" x 12" purchased pillow insert

1/2 yd. 1" grid paper (or rotary cutter and mat)

Matching thread

Iron

Note: 1/2" seam allowance included.

MAKING PATTERN PIECE

1. Pillow Front and Back: Using 1" grid paper, cut a 13" x 13" square.

Note: If you own a rotary cutter and mat, you can cut the fabric without making a pattern.

CUTTING THE PIECES

2. Using the pattern, out of dupioni silk, cut two pieces.

3. Baste the Kente strip in place on the front of one piece.

4. Baste the decorative trim over the lower edge of the strip. Stitch the trim in place.

5. With right sides together, stitch the pillow front and back together, leaving a 6" opening in the bottom.

6. Turn the pillow to the right side. Press. Insert the pillow form.

7. Slipstitch the bottom opening closed.

Project 11   Placemats

Difficulty Level: Easy

*W*ax and fancy prints are good fabrics to use for placemats; they are bright and cheerful, and they stand up to repeated washing. You can make them as simple or elaborate as you wish. These fancy prints placemats have a Kente-inspired design and make an inviting breakfast table. They would also look great on a summer barbecue buffet table.

Photo by Kim Johnson.

You will need
(for six placemats)

1 yd. fancy or wax prints

1 yd. contrasting cotton for back

1 yd. fusible low-loft batting

9 yd. matching or contrasting double-fold wide purchased bias tape

1/2 yd. 1" grid paper

Matching thread

Contrasting thread (for quilting)

Note: 1/2" seam allowance included.

MAKING THE PATTERN

1. Using 1" grid paper, cut a 12" x 15" rectangle. Round off the corners, if desired.

CUTTING THE PATTERN PIECES

2. Cut 6 front pieces from fancy or wax prints.

3. Cut 6 back pieces from contrasting cotton.

4. Cut 6 pieces from batting.

ASSEMBLING THE PLACEMATS

5. Trim off 1" from around the batting (the piece will be 11" x 14").

6. Follow the manufacturer's instructions and fuse the batting to the wrong side of the back, leaving a 1/2" area of fabric around it.

7. Pin the fancy prints or wax prints to the lining, with the wrong side against the batting. Pin in place.

8. Quilt the pieces together, using free-style quilting, lines,

or a grid pattern and the contrasting thread.

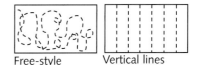

Horizontal lines   Grid

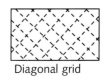

Free-style   Vertical lines

Diagonal grid

9. Encase the raw edges in bias tape. For a clean, upscale look, miter the bias at the corners. For a more casual look, attach the bias in sections. If you are making placemats with rounded edges, attach the bias in one continuous piece.

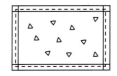

Project 12   Oven Mitt and Potholder

Difficulty Level: Easy

You Will Need
(for one oven mitt)

1/2 yd. fancy or wax prints (45" wide)

1/2 yd. canvas or heavy cotton (45" wide)

1/2 yd. high-loft batting (fusible batting optional)

1/2 yd. 1" grid or tracing paper

1 packet purchased double-fold wide bias tape

Matching thread

Contrasting thread for quilting (optional)

Photo by Kim Johnson.

We all use oven mitts and potholders, but so often they lack style. Why not make yourself a bright, cheerful set using wax or fancy prints? The cotton prints will stand up to repeated washing.

Note: 1/2" seam allowance included.

MAKING THE OVEN MITT PATTERN

1. Place your hand on the grid or tracing paper and trace the outline, leaving 2" around your hand. Extend the pattern at least 2" down your wrist.

CUTTING THE OVEN MITT PATTERN PIECES

2. Using the oven mitt pattern, cut
Two outer pieces from fancy or wax prints
Two lining pieces from cotton
Two pieces of batting

ASSEMBLING THE OVEN MITT

3. Trim off 1/2" all around the batting.

4. Baste (or fuse) the trimmed batting onto the wrong side of the canvas or heavy cotton lining.

5. Place the outer glove (print) piece over the batting, with the wrong side against the batting. Hold in place with pins. Baste. (You will sandwich the batting between the print and lining.)

6. Quilt the pieces together, using free-style quilting, lines, or a grid pattern.

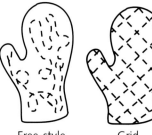

Free-style   Grid

Appendix: Fabric Summary

7. With right (print) sides together, stitch the glove pieces together, using a 1/2" seam allowance and leaving an opening 2-1/2" from the lower edge on one side.

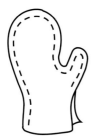

8. To make the loop, cut a 3" strip of bias tape. Stitch the open edge closed. Fold the bias strip in half to form a loop.

9. Finish the edge of the glove with the bias tape. Position the loop in the seam at the edge of the mitt, making sure all raw edges are even. Stitch the opening closed.

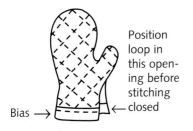

Bias →   ← closed

Position loop in this opening before stitching closed

10. Finish the seam's raw edge. Turn the mitt to the right side.

You Will Need
(for one potholder)

1/4 yd. fancy or wax prints (45" wide)

1/4 yd. canvas or heavy cotton (45" wide)

1/4 yd. high-loft batting (fusible batting optional)

1/4 yd. 1" grid or tracing paper

1 packet purchased double-fold wide bias tape

Matching thread

Contrasting thread for quilting (optional)

Note: 1/2" seam allowance included.

CUTTING THE POTHOLDER PATTERN PIECES

1. Cut two 9" x 9" squares from the fancy or wax prints, one 9" x 9" square from the batting, and 1-1/4 yd. bias tape. You can round the corners.

ASSEMBLING THE POTHOLDER

2. Trim off 1/2" all around the batting.

3. With wrong sides together, place the batting between the two outer pieces. Pin in place. (You will "sandwich" the batting between the print and lining.)

4. Quilt the squares together, using free-style quilting, lines, or a grid pattern.

Free-style

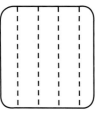

Vertical lines

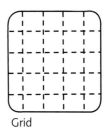

Grid

Diagonal grid

5. Finish the raw edges with bias tape. Make a loop at the end of the tape and stitch in place. Cut off any excess tape.

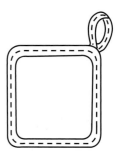

Project 13   Apron

Difficulty Level: Easy

You'll look great when you cook up a sumptuous meal in a cheerful apron (shown on page 132). This apron is easy to make and will keep your clothes spotless as you chop, dice, sauté, and blend. Make this apron to coordinate with the potholder and oven mitt, Project 12, for fashionable kitchen wear.

You Will Need

1-1/2 yd. fancy or wax prints (45" wide)

Matching thread

Tape measure

Iron

Serger (optional)

CUTTING THE PIECES

1. Cut three strips, 45" long by 2-1/2" wide, from the fancy or wax prints.

2. Measure your bustline, and divide this measurement by four. Note this length as A.

3. Measure the length from your bustline to your waistline. Note this length as B.

4. Measure your waistline, and divide this measurement by four. Note this length as C.

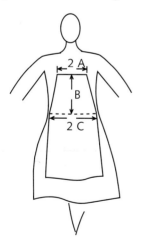

5. Fold the remaining fabric in half.

6. Measure the lengths A, B, and C on the fabric as shown. Cut out the apron piece.

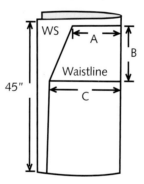

ASSEMBLING THE APRON

7. Press under 1/2" along the length of each strip from Step 1.

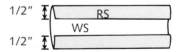

8. Fold each strip in half along the length and press.

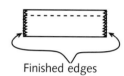

9. Stitch the strips along the length and finish the short sides' raw edges with a zigzag or serger.

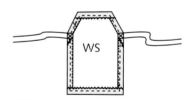

10. Finish the apron's edges with a zigzag or serger.

11. Fold under and press down the finished edges 1". Stitch the edges in place.

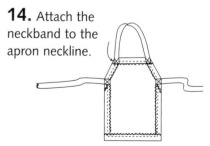

12. Attach two straps at the waistline (join of B and C).

13. Using the third strip, measure and cut off a comfortable length for the neckband. Finish the raw edges of the strip with a zigzag or serger.

14. Attach the neckband to the apron neckline.

Project 14   Build a Child's Loom

Difficulty Level: Easy to Intermediate

African children start learning to weave Korhogo cloth, Kente cloth, and mudcloth at very young ages. They even build their own looms! Now you and your children can build one, too. With this simple loom, you can make some very nice strips, even with inlaid motifs. Don't get too hung up on details as you work on this project. Children exhibit incredible creative intuition with it, figuring out ways to change designs and create inlaid motifs. Nothing is "wrong" in this creative learning process. For a visual explanation for weaving, see the accompanying video to Master Weaver from Ghana, by Louise Meyer and "Bobbo" Gilbert Ahiagble (see Bibliography).

You Will Need

3 dowels, 6" long x 1/4" diameter

1 chopstick or 1/8" round metal rod

2 ice cream sticks or tongue depressors

Cotton thread (mercerized, preferably) or thin, strong packaging string in the colors of your choice

Wooden base (optional)

Wood glue

Comb

Pencil

Drill and 1/8" and 1/4" drill bits (optional)

Instructions courtesy of Louise Meyer, www.africancrafts.com

1. Mark the positions for the dowels in a triangle arrangement on the ground or on the wooden base to the following positions: Two dowels will be at a distance of 8" for the back of the loom and one

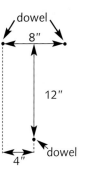

centered between these two, 12" away (see also the photo of the loom on page 50).

2. On two of the dowels, mark a line 1/2" from an edge. Using string, attach the chopstick or metal rod (this will be the cross-stick), horizontally, close to the tops of the two vertical dowels.

Optional: Drill a hole through the dowels at this position. You will place the chopstick or metal rod through this hole to attach to the vertical dowels.

3. Push the dowels into the ground, forming a triangle. If you are using the wooden base, you can simply glue the dowels onto the base, forming the triangle. You can also drill small holes (using the 1/4" drill bit) into the wooden base at the triangle positions and glue the dowels into these holes.

4. Wrap thread around the front dowel and bring it up and over the cross stick and back around the front dowel until 15 to 20 threads are laid out at even distances from one another, forming a warp.

5. Make a shuttle using an ice cream stick or a tongue depressor to hold the cross thread, the weft, which will go over and under the individual warp threads at right angles. To make the shuttle, simply wrap a good length of string (1 to 2 yards) around the ice cream stick.

6. Use the other ice cream stick or tongue depressor to separate odd warp threads from even warp threads to prepare an opening (a shed) through which the shuttle holding the weft thread can pass. Pass the shuttle through the shed. Pack the new weft thread into the warp with your fingers or a comb.

7. Now separate the opposite set of threads in the warp (odd from even) to create a second opening (shed) to make a new passage for the second weft thread, pack down tightly toward the first weft thread.

8. Continue, by repeating Steps 5, 6, and 7.

CHANGING COLORS

To add another color, simply wrap another shuttle with the color you want to add and repeat Steps 5, 6, and 7 using the new color until you build up as much of the new color as you like. (Optional) You do not have to completely finish one shuttle to add another color. You can work several colors at the same time, passing the different colored shuttles as you need them. Leave the shuttles attached and off to the side as you work with a new color. Pick up different colors as you desire.

MAKING DESIGNS AND INLAID MOTIFS

You use a pick-up technique to make inlaid motifs. Use your fingers to pick up one thread of the warp and let rest three and repeat across the entire warp or only over a portion of it (you can vary the number of threads you pick up). Then, place a pick-up stick in that space to hold it open; next, the weft (often shiny rayon thread is used here) is put into that space (use another shuttle or single threads). This is done again and again to put in the inlaid motif, but each special insertion of inlaid is held in place (tacked down, so to speak) by one shot (entry) of a normal weft on the shuttle (which is still attached). Pick up your normal shuttle once you complete the inlaid motif.

ENDING THE WEFT THREAD

You end these different colored weft picks (entries) by breaking the weft thread and leaving it half-way through the warp and placing the new color on top of it (or inside the same opening, which is called a shed).

Samples courtesy Louise Meyer.

Strips woven by children in Korhogo.

FABRIC KEY

Fabric Characteristics

- **Mudcloth** — Fairly stable cloth out of narrow strips sewn together, visually rugged, decorated with natural dyes.
- **Korhogo Cloth** — Fairly stable cloth out of narrow strips sewn together, visually rugged, decorated with natural dyes.
- **Kuba Cloth** — Hand woven (sometimes irregular shaped) raffia cloth, decorated with appliqués, tie-dye, and plush.
- **Kente Cloth** — Hand woven cloth out of narrow strips sewn together. Ashanti Kente is characterized by bright colors woven in geometric motifs. Ewe Kente is woven in subtle colors with inlaid motifs of everyday items, i.e., chairs, keys, etc. Cotton, silk, rayon, or synthetic yarns are used.
- **Wax and Fancy Prints** — Factory produced cotton fabrics, printed and dyed with "African-influenced" motifs. Wax prints are printed on both sides. Fancy prints are printed on one side.

Works Well With

Fabric	Linen	Hemp	Mudcloth	Dupioni Silk	Raw Silk	Wool Crepe	Satin	Jute	Korhogo Cloth	Canvas	Cotton	Suede	Leather
Mudcloth	X	X			X	X		X	X	X	X	X	X
Korhogo Cloth	X	X	X		X	X		X		X	X	X	
Kuba Cloth	X	X		X							X	X	X
Kente Cloth	X	X		X	X		X	X		X	X	X	X
Wax and Fancy Prints	X	X		X	X		X				X		

Design Ideas

Fabric	Dresses	Blouses	Shirts	Suits	Jackets	Coats	Children's Clothes	Bags	Decorative Trims	Placemats	Wall Hangings	Pillows	Crafts
Mudcloth	X			X	X	X	X	X	X	X	X	X	X
Korhogo Cloth	X			X	X	X	X	X	X		X	X	X
Kuba Cloth				X	X	X		X	X	X	X	X	X
Kente Cloth	X	X			X	X	X	X	X	X	X	X	X
Wax and Fancy Prints	X	X	X	X	X	X	X	X	X	X		X	X

Resources

Museums and Other Expert Fabric Advice

Afrograph. Specializes in wax prints, African cottons, and Kente cloth. Provides consulting services to museums, cultural, and other organizations. Fabric collection available for loan.
49 Forest Road
Prenton, Liverpool,
Merseyside, U.K. CH43 1UH
0151-652-9512
Fax: 0151-652-9512
e-mail: afrograph@freeuk.com

Aid to Artisans. Non-profit organization that helps artisans around the world bring their products to market through training, market development, and matchmaking with buyers.
14 Brick Walk Lane
Farmington, CT 06032
860-677-1649
www.aid2artisans.org

Fowler Museum of African Art. Extensive collection of African textiles and research materials.
Box 951549
Los Angeles, CA 90095
310-825-4361
www.fmch.ucla.edu

Kente Cloth Festival. Historical information on Ashanti Kente cloth, with a wide selection available for purchase. Custom-sewing also available. Organizes the annual Kente Cloth Festival in August in New York.
Contact: Bosompim Kusi.
718-588-3502
www.kente.net

National Museum of African Art, Smithsonian Institution. Extensive collection of African textiles and research materials.
950 Independence Ave., SW
Washington, D.C. 20560
202-357-4600
www.si.edu/nmafa

The Pyramid Complex. Specializes in mudcloth and adinkra cloth.
Contact: Bruce Willis, author of *The Adinkra Dictionary*
P.O. Box 21212
Washington, D.C. 20009
202-332-3908

Sankofa Educultural Consultants.
Contact: Dr. Kwaku Ofori-Ansa, professor and consultant on African Art and Cultural Education, and expert on Ashanti Kente
2211 Amherst Rd.
Hyattsville, MD 20783
301-422-0540

School of Oriental and African Studies (SOAS) Expert advice on African textiles.
University of London
Thornhaugh St. Russell Square
London WC1H0XG, U.K.
0207-323-6282
www.soas.ac.uk

Textile Museum Good collection of Kuba cloth and other African textiles. Research materials available.
2320 S St., NW
Washington, D.C. 20008
202-667-0441
Fax: 202-483-0994
www.textilemuseum.org

Fabric Care

International Fabricare Institute Membership association for professional dry cleaners and laundries that provides advice and has booklets on care methods for some African fabrics. Better dry cleaners are IFI members.
12251 Tech Road
Silver Spring, MD 20904
301-622-1900
www.ifi.org

For more information, contact the museums listed at left.

Fabrics: Mail-order, Internet Sources, Store Locations, Wholesale, and Retail

Note: Also check your local Jo-Ann Fabrics and Crafts and Hancock Fabrics for African fabrics.

A. Brunnschweiler & Company (ABC Wax). Wholesale and Internet retail. Wax prints manufacturer. Distributors around the world listed.
www.abcwax.co.uk

Adire African Textiles. Internet retail. Author Duncan Clarke's website. Excellent collection of Ewe Kente, Kuba cloth, mudcloth, and other African textiles.
Portobello Road Market
W. Jones Arcade
113 Portobello Rd.
London W11, U.K.
0410-791-497
www.adire.clara.net

Afritex. Wholesale. Fancy prints and mudcloth.
350 7th Ave., Suite 1701
New York, NY 10001
1-888-9AFRITEX
www.afritex.com

Artifactory. Retail. Great selection of Kuba cloth, Ashanti Kente cloth, Korhogo cloth, and mudcloth.
641 Indiana Ave., NW
Washington, D.C. 20004
202-393-2727.

Cy Rudnik Fabrics. Retail store. Mudcloth and African cotton prints.
2450 Grand Ave.
Kansas City, MO 64108
816-842-7808.

ebay. Internet auction site where you can bid for fabrics.
www.ebay.com

G Street Fabrics. Retail store and Internet source. Fancy prints, wax prints, Korhogo cloth, and mudcloth. Three outlets:
11854 Rockville
Pike, MD 20852
301-231-8998

5077 Westfilds Blvd.
Centreville, VA 20120
703-818-8090

6250 Seven Corners
Falls Church, VA 22044
703-241-1700
www.gstreetfabrics.com

Homeland Authentics. Wholesale and retail. Mail-order catalog. Fancy prints and mudcloth. Swatch books available.
122 W 27th St.
New York, NY 10001
1-800-AFRICAN

International Fabric Collection. Retail and mail-order. Mudcloth, wax and fancy prints.
3445 West Lake Rd.
Erie, PA 16505
814-838-0740
www.intfab.com

Kaarta Imports. Wholesale and retail. Wide selection of mudcloth and Korhogo cloth.
121 W 125th St.
New York, NY 10027
212-866-5190

Miya Gallery. Retail. Specializes in mudcloth, Korhogo cloth, and Kuba cloth. Good selection of unusual pieces.
629 E St., NW
Washington, D.C. 20004
202-347-6330
www.artobjects.com
e-mail: nsagi@interchange.org

Quilts 'N Stuff. Retail. Good collection of Kuba cloth and other African fabrics. Quilting supplies and ideas for quilting with African fabrics.
5962 Richmond Hwy.
Alexandria, VA 22303
703-836-0070
e-mail: ansi@erols.com

St. Teresa Textile Trove. Retail. Mudcloth and fancy prints.
1329 Main St.
Cincinnati, OH 45210
513-333-0399

Union des Groupements à Vocation Coopérative d'Artisans du Nord (UGAN). Retail and wholesale cooperative of Korhogo cloth artisans.
Boîte Postale 163
Korhogo, Côte d'Ivoire
Tel/Fax 225 86 03 19

West Africa Imports. Wholesale and Retail. Internet source. Wide selection of Kuba cloth, mudcloth, Korhogo cloth, and fancy prints.
www.africanimports.com

Sewing Patterns

Hibiscus Patterns. Sewing patterns featuring modern designs for ethnic fabrics including mudcloth, fancy prints, and Korhogo cloth.
Contact: RL Boone
P.O. Box 3276
Falls Church, VA 22304
703-448-3884
www.Hibiscus.net
e-mail:
RLBoone@RLBoone.com

Folkwear Patterns. Offers patterns of traditional ethnic costumes.
67 Broadway
Asheville, NC 28801
1-800-284-3388
www.larkbooks.com

Ofa Patterns. Sewing patterns of traditional African attire.
Contact: Akwele El
4929 Arctic Terrace
Rockville, MD 20853
301-929-2697

Ethnic-influenced Buttons

Curran Square Fabrics. Retail store.
6825 Redmond Dr.
McLean, VA 22101
703-556-9292

The Button Shoppe. Mail-order. Catalog available.
4744 Oakfield Circle
Carmichael, CA 95608
916-488-5350

Designers and Artisans

Thony Anyiams. Bridal and special occasion fashions from African fabrics.
www.anyiams.com

Dominick Cardella, Owner, Artifactory. Contemporary and traditional attire out of mudcloth, Kente cloth, and cotton prints.
641 Indiana Ave., NW
Washington, D.C. 20004

Nestor Hernandez, Atlas Upholstery. Upholsters furniture with African fabrics.
5401 Annapolis Rd.
Bladensburg, MD 20710
301-864-3300

Louise Meyer. Custom-made placemats and vertical blinds using Ewe Kente and Korhogo cloth.
www.africancrafts.com

Lisa Shepard. Custom-made home furnishings and attire. Author of *African Accents*.
www.culturedexpressions.com

Brenda Winstead, Owner, Damali Afrikan Wear. High-fashion, art-to-wear clothing featuring mudcloth, Kuba cloth, and other African fabrics.
1309 Q St., NW
Washington, D.C. 20009
202-234-4427
e-mail:
damaliafrikanwear@msn.com

Workshops/Classes

Aba Tours and African Crafts Online. Organize Kente weaving study tours to Ghana. Course participants study under master weavers, developing skills and learning about the history and cultural significance of Kente in Ghana.
617-277-0482 or 202-328-6834
e-mail:
abatours@africancrafts.com **or** louise@africancrafts.com
www.africancrafts.com

Fiber City Sewing. Offers various classes.
775 West Jackson Blvd.
Chicago, IL 60661
312-648-0954

G Street Fabrics. Catalog of workshops available.
301-231-8998
www.gstreetfabrics.com

RLBoone. Offers workshops and classes on designing and sewing modern fashions with African textiles. Group and private classes available.
703-448-3884
www.Hibiscus.net
e-mail:
RLBoone@RLBoone.com

Related Web Sites

African Crafts Online. Showcases the work of artisans, designers, and educators working with African fabrics and ornaments. Resource for educational information for school programs, including book and companion video *Master Weaver from Ghana*, by Gilbert "Bobbo" Ahiagble, Louise Meyer, and Nestor Hernandez.
www.africancrafts.com

Ashanti Origins. Beautiful custom art furniture, including pieces upholstered with mudcloth, Korhogo cloth, and other African textiles.
56 Lafayette Ave.
Brooklyn, NY 11217
718-855-1006
www.ashantiorigins.com

Bibliography

Adams, Moni. "Kuba Embroidered Cloth." *African Arts* 12 (1): pp. 24-39, 106, 1978.

Billings, Kathy. "The Kasai Velvets. A Decorative Art Form of the Bakuba." *The Arts of Black Africa*, Fall 1977.

Clarke, Duncan. *The Art of African Textiles*. San Diego, CA: Thunder Bay Press. 1977.

Hollis, Sara. "Shoowa Textiles from the Kingdom of Kuba in Zaire." *Arts Quarterly* (New Orleans) 10 (3): pp. 10-12, July-September 1988.

Imperato, Pascal James. "Bokolanfini. Mud Cloth of the Bamana of Mali." *African Arts*, pp. 32-41, 80, Summer 1970.

Mack, John. "In Search of the Abstract." *Hali: The International Magazine of Antiques, Carpets and Textiles* (London), 8 (3) no. 31: pp 26-33, 103 July-September 1986.

Meurant, George. *Shoowa Design*. London: Thames and Hudson. 1986.

Meyer, Louise and "Bobbo" Gilbert Ahiagble. *Master Weaver from Ghana*. Washington, D.C.: Open Hand Publishing. 1998.

National Museum of African Art. *Discover Shoowa Design, Gallery Activities for Children and Adults*, Washington, D.C.

Polakoff, Claire. *Into Indigo*. New York: Anchor Books. 1980.

Picton, John and John Mack. *African Textiles. Looms, Weaving and Design*, British Museum Publications for The Trustees of the British Museum, London, 1979.

Ross, Doran H. et. al. *Wrapped in Pride. Ghanian Kente and African American Identity*, UCLA Fowler Museum of Cultural History and the Newark Museum, 1998.

Svenson, Anne E. "Kuba Textiles: An Introduction." *WAAC Newsletter*, Volume 8, Number 1: pp. 2-5, Jan. 1986.

——"Kuba Textiles: An Introduction to Raffia Textiles." The Conservation Center, Los Angeles County Museum of Art, Textile Conservation Symposium in honor of Pat Reeves, 58-62, 1986.

Thomas, Wendy Anne. "The Role of Woven and Embroidered Textiles of the Bakuba: Visual and Historical Dimensions." *Master of the Arts Thesis*, York University, 1983.

Index

And the drums played all night
And they danced by the sea
A quilt of people
Twirling and moving to the beat.

Flashes of fabric
Exotic colors and prints
A dancing rainbow
Enjoying life's beat.

And in the silver moonlight
Their style shone thru'
Each different, each beautiful to behold!

So dance where you are
Dance to life's beat
Seek nature's colors and prints.
Twinkle. Be radiant, beautiful in all that
    you do
And your style will shine thru' day by day.

And the drums played all night
And they danced by the sea
A quilt of people
Twirling and moving to the beat.

Flashes of fabric
Exotic colors and prints
A dancing rainbow
Enjoying life's beat.

And in the silver moonlight
Their style shone thru'
Each different, each beautiful to behold!

So dance where you are
Dance to life's beat
Seek nature's colors and prints.
Twinkle. Be radiant, beautiful in all that
    you do
And your style will shine thru' day by day.